"I am myn owene woman, wel at ese"

In Memory of Margaret Jennings

"I am myn owene woman, wel at ese"
In Memory of Margaret Jennings

CONTRIBUTIONS BY

Francis P. Kilcoyne, Mary Florence Burns, C.S.J., Eugene Crook, Michael Haren, and Siegfried Wenzel

WITH MARGARET JENNINGS'S ESSAY

"Eyewitness: Ranulph Higden and the Troubling Events
at Chester Monastery"

PEETERS
LEUVEN - PARIS - BRISTOL, CT
2017

Cover illustration: The quotation is from Geoffrey Chaucer, *Troilus and Criseyde*, Book II, line 750. Calligraphy by Steve Czajka, Toronto.

A catalogue record for this book is available from the Library of Congress.

© 2017 – Peeters – Bondgenotenlaan 153 – B-3000 Leuven – Belgium.
ISBN 978-90-429-3494-8
D/2017/0602/59

Professor Margaret Jennings

Table of Contents

Margaret Jennings Kilcoyne
(August 29, 1942–August 26, 2016)
The Woman of a Thousand Welcomes

By Francis P. Kilcoyne

Scholars familiar with Margaret's academic interests and skill set might well describe her in the classical sense as a woman of many parts. Scholars, former students, and her numerous friends who gathered at St. Augustine's Church, Brooklyn, for the Mass of the Resurrection on Labor Day weekend, 2016, revealed that she was a woman of many constituencies. In each of these she was remarkably involved, and friends both admired and were amused at the ease with which she morphed from one to the next. How characterize this life?

As I reflect on her engagement as wife, neighbor, friend, teacher, and scholar, the common thread which emerges is the attitude of welcome. While she had little patience with the Irish Tourist Board's sentimentalizing of "The Land of a Thousand Welcomes," Margaret's incarnation of welcome had a very Irish dimension, rooted as it was in her family's warm spirit of engagement, boundless hospitality, and uplifting embrace of the guest's story—regardless of whether the guest was young or old, an acquaintance of long standing or newly arrived, of exalted pedigree or neophyte. Individuals were accepted on the merit of their own interests and needs. When Margaret spoke with you, it was an unconditional encounter. There was never a sense that she was looking over your shoulder to see if a more significant or interesting prospect was on the horizon. She always conveyed the sense that what the other brought to the conversation enhanced her worldview and merited a thoughtful response. As that atmosphere of welcome permeated subsequent encounters, there emerged the opportunity to explore more deeply whatever was being discussed. Putting people at ease and fostering curiosity and confidence to grow in understanding were a hallmark of Margaret's spirit of welcoming into her many worlds. Throughout, her primary mode of punctuation was her hearty smile and infectious laughter, as often as not directed at herself. This whole living process was meant to be enjoyable!

Her constituencies ranged wide, and each experienced this welcoming encouragement. Friends of long standing in the scholarly community were Gene Crook and Michael Haren. Although they were geographically dispersed, regular phone and email contact fostered a warm, supportive, and productive relationship. "These are the guys I can always count on"—and their periodic messages always brightened her day.

The community of St. Joseph's College, Brooklyn, was a forty-five-year anchor in her life. Particularly close was Sr. Florence Burns, C.S.J., friend and supportive interlocutor. Long-time faculty were her sounding board in the world of ideas and personal life as was she for them. Younger faculty regularly sought her perceptive insight, gentle nudge, and dismissal of self-pity. Within two weeks of a semester she knew every student by name, and their interests and needs received regular attention. The daughter of immigrants, she welcomed those recently arrived in America and the even more numerous students who were the first in their families to attend college.

A Russian émigrée whose only association with her Jewish roots was a specific last name which invited discrimination at the University of Moscow inquired about the significance of all the medieval allusions to this collection called the Bible. Margaret worked up a private introduction to the Hebrew Bible for one hour a week for a semester. She learned Spanish to better work with Latina students or, more specifically, their parents, who were skeptical about the wisdom of supporting their daughters' college aspirations in this new Anglo world. The inner city affords its own walls of isolation and insecurity. Seldom did students in her advanced classes escape the expansive encounter of research assignments rooted in one of New York City's gems of scholarship, the library at Forty-Second Street and Fifth Avenue. Of course, accompanying this trial by fire was a ten-point guide on how to penetrate the library's arcane mysteries. Eventually librarians who spotted students with the one-page guide extended the greeting, "Oh, you must be from St. Joseph's."

Her offices in Brooklyn and later in Chestnut Hill had an open-door policy. It was a frequent site of faculty exchanges. Supportive and constructive critique often strengthened the faint of heart and calmed many a tempest in a teapot.

In 1988 marriage presented a new challenge: where to call home, and how to live the rest of the time. For home, the 1850s cottage in Framingham won the day. Then the question, Why rent an apartment if you will only be in it seventy-five days a year. A Winnebago was not the answer. After residing with a friend for a few semesters, Margaret rented a room for twenty years with Hour Children, a residential program conducted by the Sisters of St. Joseph for women convicts who had babies in jail and were about to be paroled. In this environment, welcome took on new meaning. Every morning at 5:30 a.m. while having her breakfast Margaret would spread out the circulars from Framingham supermarkets and discuss with the residents, also up and getting ready for their jobs or training programs, how to plan a weekly menu, avoid impulse buying, and stretch the budget. Also discussed were savings plans and educational aspirations for their children. Welcome to the real world's nitty-gritty! After that workshop it was off to St. Joseph's.

Welcome is not a greeting celebrated on an empty stomach. In her successive residences in Brooklyn a steady flow of students were treated to good food and long evenings of conversation. Special guests included Dante and Chaucer! During the twenty years she commuted weekly from our home in Framingham, Massachusetts, to Brooklyn every Monday, returning on Thursday, she developed a meals-on-wheels approach. Food prepared in Massachusetts arrived in Brooklyn and was devoured around her office conference table. Somehow, Mr. Alighieri and Geoff continued to appear! At the same time, for over twenty-five years we entertained about two thousand students from Boston College and Harvard at similar evening events in Framingham. Conversations always ranged into the night. Again, those two old guys showed up, along with a Brit named Ranulph!

Young neighbors in Framingham sought Margaret's guidance and were favored by a good listener, encouraging insights, and creative support in life and career values and choices. One young man who had enjoyed his high school Latin honors experience inquired how he could learn Anglo-Saxon. His summer was highlighted by a two-month tutorial running through basic grammar, vocabulary, and selected readings.

Margaret's capacity for welcome was not limited to the collegiate world. Much advice was shared in the areas of gardening, sewing, and home improvement. Of her gardening she observed, "Not bad for a city girl!" One Jewish neighbor who had been raised outside her cooking heritage benefited from the fact that Margaret had grown up as the Irish minority in an otherwise Jewish apartment house in Brooklyn. Margaret had enthusiastically learned the preparation mysteries of blintzes, potato latke, matzo ball soup, and pickled herring. She happily welcomed our neighbor into her cooking heritage.

For Margaret, welcoming was a process intended to perdure. Over thirty years she produced as gifts more than three hundred afghans for relatives, friends, and neighbors to celebrate significant moments in their lives, going to or graduating from college, getting married, having a baby. She hoped that the warmth of the blanket enhanced the memory of previous conversations and supportive anecdotes.

While Margaret shunned the combative, she never ran from issues of justice when principle was involved. She learned much of this from her father, a former IRA commandant in County Mayo and twenty-year veteran of the NYPD. In the 1916 Easter Rising he declined a royal scholarship to Cambridge, enlisting instead in the fight for Irish freedom. In the 1950s, unlike many Brooklyn Irish Catholics, he staunchly defended his Jewish neighbors against the anti-Semitic and Red-baiting agenda of the local Catholic newspaper, which sought to align American Catholicism with the rancorous oratory of a junior senator from Wisconsin. Margaret's sense of just welcome motivated her to volunteer her teaching services for two summers at the Wounded Knee Reservation, to support fair housing initiatives in central Brooklyn, and it energized her opposition to a Framingham bigot hostile to recently arrived Brazilians.

Certain issues she viewed as merely pathetic, and these were greeted with a disbelieving shake of the head. As an early member of the translation team of the International Commission for English in the Liturgy (ICEL), which translated the Roman Missal after Vatican II, she viewed the most recent effort as inhospitable to adult speakers of twenty-first-century English. Frequently she observed, "Bad Latin, worse English, and unfortunate pastoral and liturgical scholarship."

One of the blessings which we shared was that our academic fields of interest overlapped. Church history, liturgical theology, and archaeological work in the Eastern Mediterranean were my foci. Margaret loved her manuscript work and, more recently, her art historical studies. Cathedrals from Trondheim in Norway to Monreale, Sicily, focused her inquiry. Her scope was broadened by the painted churches of Meteora and Kastoria in Greece and the rural villages of Cyprus. She enthusiastically climbed the endless stairs to the monasteries at Meteora, the subterranean chambers of the valleys of Selime and Göreme, and visited some of the more rustic Greek sites by motorcycle!

Her sense of incarnation in the concrete was informed by her extensive research on local church experience, as distinct from the university centers of Paris, Bologna, and Oxford. The local church offered a different perspective of the Word becoming flesh than that of the schoolmen. Higden confronted the faith community in terms of his abiding belief in a saving God present in Word, Sacrament, and community. Yet the general social disarray, particularly after the Black Death, combined with the experience of the local monastery in the grip of dissolute, homicidal abbots. Margaret was not overly surprised by current revelations of ecclesiastical blemishes. She observed that if God had wanted perfect he would not have chosen flesh but rather marble, gold, or platinum. But He did choose flesh, warts and all, and invited His communities to accept the invitation to make the Word flesh and to nourish that process themselves as body of Christ, warts and all, to be broken and given.

Margaret viewed her role as teacher, scholar, and friend as one whereby through dedication, critical thinking, personal warmth, and welcoming engagement she was able to make the realities, hopes, and insights of another age alive and effective in the present day. For many years she taught an intensive course on *La Divina Comedia* during Holy Week, culminating with the invitation to her students to participate in the Great Vigil of Easter: not a bad window into Dante, his appreciation of the Christian community, warts and all, then and now.

A week before she died, quite peacefully she reflected that she had enjoyed a full, rewarding and enjoyable life. Chaucer well phrased it, "I am myn owene woman, wel at ese." The Irish verse on her memorial card reads: "Grieve not ... nor speak of me with tears ... but laugh and talk of me as though I were beside you. I loved you so 'twas heaven here with you."

Gaude et laetare

By Sr. Mary Florence Burns, C.S.J.

How capture the spirit of Margaret Jennings Kilcoyne, a woman of tremendous capabilities and wide interests, a woman who literally could turn her head and her hand from the home-made soup on the stove to a troublesome Latin translation? A woman whose head and heart captured each one of us, and who brings us together in celebration of a life that brought joy into each one of our lives.

It all began in Brooklyn, New York, with a very intelligent young woman, beloved daughter of Mary and John Jennings, immigrants from Ireland, who set the example of love of God and neighbor, and of independent thinking. Indeed, her father had forfeited a royal scholarship to Cambridge, and risked his life, when he joined the Irish Rising in 1916. Here he served on the side of law and order as a member of the New York City Police Department.

With a New York State Regents Scholarship, Margaret attended St. Joseph's College for one year, then, with her parents' consent, left to join the Sisters of St. Joseph, Brentwood, in 1960. Her academic record at Brentwood College led to a Woodrow Wilson Fellowship to the University of North Carolina, Chapel Hill, where Siegfried Wenzel recognized her ability and supported her application for a doctoral fellowship to Bryn Mawr. There Myra Uhlfelder directed her work. These mentors in the medieval field recognized her brilliance, and in the years that followed, their sponsorship led to additional scholarships and opportunities for research in Toronto, Munich, Heidelberg, the Vatican Library, and the Bodleian Library at Oxford, as well as time at Harvard, St. Louis, and New York University. In return she presented regularly at academic conferences such as the Modern Language Association and the Medieval Academy of America, authored more than forty scholarly papers, and almost incidentally served on ICEL, the International Commission on English in the Liturgy. After editing the Troilus text in the *Riverside Chaucer*, she undertook her major work, completed in June, 2016: the edition and translation, with Eugene Crook, of Ranulph Higden's fourteenth-century, four-volume, 1,500-page handbook for curates. In the thickets of a medieval manual, Margaret found insights into the lives of ordinary people in the fourteenth century.

All of this is impressive in its own right. What is astonishing is everything else she was doing at the same time. As a Sister of St. Joseph, she came to St. Joseph's College in 1969, doctorate completed, degree awarded in 1970. That is when she and I met. I had just been appointed academic dean of the small liberal-arts college. Margaret came to take my program, in its own way an inauspicious beginning. I loved teaching. My own doctoral work in medieval studies at Columbia had been under Roger Sherman Loomis and Elliot Van Kirk Dobbie, but that was a generation earlier. Margaret wanted her independence and no advice. With the ground rules established, and with somewhat open minds on both sides, we soon came to an understanding that developed over the years into real friendship.

From the beginning, Margaret taught four courses each semester: initially the traditional British survey courses, composition, Chaucer, and medieval literature. In later years, with curricular changes, she added courses in short story, classics in English, continental masterworks, modern American drama, modern European drama, thesis for English majors, and, on the side, supervised student teachers. In 1971, when St. Joseph's College began to develop the Long Island campus, first in Brentwood, then in Patchogue, 63 miles away, Margaret made regular trips to teach there as well. In one semester, against all protocol, she taught six courses, and on the annual faculty resume she wrote, "Never again!"

Margaret and a sister in the History Department organized and co-directed an annual ten-day study trip to England for students and alumni throughout the 1970s—in the raw cold of January because, of course, it was significantly less expensive and not at all crowded. Based in Oxford, the groups traveled out by bus to Stonehenge and Bath, then spent a few days in London, with side-trip to Canterbury. Lunch was on the bus, but afternoon tea was occasionally permitted as culturally important.

Faculty and administrators came to recognize her organizational ability and political acumen. Margaret never wanted administration, but over the years, she co-chaired two Middle States self-studies, chaired the English Department, and chaired the Committee on Rank, Tenure, and Faculty interests—never her favorite, but never a complaint, either. An academic vice president's dream faculty member.

At the heart of her academic career, however, were the students—the really gifted, whose careers she fostered, and the ordinary, whose interests she piqued and expanded. Highly organized and quite demanding, she communicated such enthusiasm that she persuaded students that they would understand and enjoy medieval texts. So they did. For years she taught the first half of the senior survey and guided seniors, on both campuses, in designing their theses. She also created cassette courses for summer study; over time, these morphed into online courses. For seniors who suddenly discovered that they were three credits short for graduation, they were what the dean called "emergency parachutes." Margaret herself called them "drama for the desperate." Her goal was to enable students to develop to their full capacity—by whatever means. Like Chaucer's clerk of Oxenford, "Gladly would she learn and gladly teach." Her impact was enormous.

When, in 1986, it was clear to her that religious life was not her real calling, with characteristic honesty she made the decision to move in a different direction. The decision was not sudden. Margaret had entered the convent in 1960, a very stable time in the Catholic Church in the United States. By the mid-1960s, the country was experiencing radical change: the assassination of John F. Kennedy, the social upheaval and civil rights progress under Lyndon Johnson, the war in Vietnam, the student revolution at Berkeley, with repercussions throughout higher education— and for Catholics and religious in particular, Pope John XXIII and Vatican II. Sr. Margaret Jennings came to St. Joseph's College in 1969, one of four young sisters, newly or nearly minted PhDs, coming like young Turks into a conventional setting of some forty well-educated sisters of a wide age range who were at various political, social, and religious points in their lives. Within a few years, the young sisters received permission to form a separate community just a block away. By the early 1980s, Margaret requested exclaustration, lived in a small apartment for a few years, and then in 1986 was dispensed from her vows. The internal struggle of this period never affected her teaching or her relationships with other sisters.

And somewhat later, God blessed her with Francis Patrick Kilcoyne, Jr. Pat Kilcoyne's mother was chair of the Physical Education Department at Brooklyn College of the City University of New York, an impressive position for a woman at that time. His father was a faculty member, later dean, ultimately president of Brooklyn College. As a young teacher, Dr. Kilcoyne, Sr., taught as an adjunct at St. Joseph's College, and brought young Pat as a four-year old to the College's Dillon Child Study Center, a laboratory pre-school. The connection with St. Joseph's College ran through two generations. And in the neighborhood ways of Brooklyn, Margaret and Pat knew of each other but had had no social connection. In 1986, at the very time that Margaret left the convent, Pat Kilcoyne was in the process of relocating to Boston College. Against this background, Margaret and Pat met in the most romantic of settings—the catalog section of the New York University library. *Mirabile dictu*: the sparks did not ignite the catalog cards. Margaret and Pat were married in 1988.

Margaret's new life did not end her ties with the Sisters of St. Joseph or St. Joseph's College. In the years of living in Framingham, Massachusetts, and commuting to Long Island to teach, she stayed with the Sisters of St. Joseph. One of our ministries is called Hour Children, a program that provides care for children of incarcerated women, who are permitted an hour's visit with their children, and transitional group housing when the mothers are paroled. Margaret was as comfortable with the women parolees and their babies as she was with the texts of St. Thomas Aquinas and Duns Scotus. And sisters and residents welcomed her laughing, joyous, helpful presence.

Finally, after forty years of remarkable service, Margaret retired from St. Joseph's College in 2009, but never really left us. She continued to teach online courses right through the spring 2016 semester. And as a capstone to her career, in a beautiful tribute, Boston College honored her with a visiting professorship, an endowed chair named for the benefactor—the Joseph Chair. Was that not appropriate? These last seven years of semi-retirement have been very special for Margaret and Pat, with Key West and New Hampshire, with Ranulph Higden always close at hand, and with beautiful, fun-filled trips to the British Isles, Italy, Israel, Greece, Cyprus and its painted churches, Anatolian Turkey, Santorini, and in June, France.

Over the years, Margaret introduced generations of students to Dante's *Divine Comedy*. If in this last year she felt, in Dante's words, that she "had strayed into a dark forest, and the right path appeared not anywhere," then, at the end of this *Purgatorio*, supported by Pat's love and strength, she came through, as Dante expresses it, "pure and disposed to mount up to the stars." She is surely living a new life, in Dante's words in the *Paradiso*, a new life "in the glory of God who moveth all that is … the Love that moves the sun and the other stars."

Pat Kilcoyne brought Margaret back to Brooklyn for the Mass of the Resurrection on Saturday of the Labor Day weekend 2016. To that Mass came theologians from Boston College, the neighbors from Framingham, old friends from Brooklyn and Queens, St. Joseph's College faculty and administrators, Sisters of St. Joseph who had entered with Margaret, and former sisters who had stayed in touch. Margaret had created community—love of God and love of neighbor—at every stage of her life. This commemorative booklet brings together the community of medievalists with whom she shared a lifelong, very special relationship. Let us give thanks for the great gift of Margaret Jennings Kilcoyne's life among us. Let us rejoice and be glad.

Margaret Jennings: A Portrait in Emails

By Eugene Crook

> "Here it is. If OK, I'll send on to Rosemann."
> — Margaret

Dated October 28, 2003, that is the earliest letter that my university's email archives have preserved from Margaret Jennings to me. It is fitting that I should start my reminiscences of Margaret with that very short note, which conveyed the attachment of our prospectus for the publication of Ranulph Higden's *Speculum curatorum* in the Dallas Medieval Texts and Translations series. Margaret had already published in that series Higden's *Ars componendi sermones* in the translation by herself and Sally A. Wilson, so she felt she had some influence with the editor. We had been writing and emailing about the proposed *Speculum* project intermittently since 1976, after Siegfried Wenzel had put us in communication because of our mutual interest in the *Speculum* (hers the earlier version, and mine the later).

While Neil Ker was a visiting professor at the University of Illinois at Urbana-Champaign in 1968, he identified the Illinois manuscript of the *Speculum* and connected it with the four known manuscripts of an earlier, shorter version that is preserved in British libraries. He subsequently recommended that I edit the work. Since I had already gathered microfilms of all the known manuscripts, I set to work transcribing the Illinois manuscript and began connecting it to the disparate passages of the earlier version. But my initial translations needed more help than I could give.

The original prospectus for Book I: *The Commandments* that Margaret had drawn up was ambitious, and the timeline was unrealistically so. I commented that I thought we could do it, even if it meant no Christmas for me. Her immediate reply: "You need to have Christmas! I'll change the timeline ... let's be realistic for a minute." Her first thoughts were always human and humane, and whatever we committed ourselves to do, it had to fit in with our other lives.

Margaret was equally aware of the many friends she had made over the years: "Michael Haren (*Memoriale presbyterorum*) is a friend of mine, and I am not averse to begging for pieces of text to enhance our discussion." Later, "I've heard from Michael Haren and Patrick Horner, so there will be good material for comparison." Margaret became friends so endearingly that everyone was eager to assist her work.

Margaret and her husband, Francis Patrick Kilcoyne, had a couple of housing options besides their small but comfortable home in Framingham, Massachusetts: "Thanks to my sainted father-in-law, Pat and I have a timeshare in Key West. What a great place!" And certainly she needed a break from the winter weather as she comments at the end of January, 2004: "At the moment I am about to free my car from a snowdrift. Enjoyment seems far away! Hope your semester is going well. Mine is literally snowbound." In my brief remarks here, I will limit myself to the year 2004, when our project got underway in earnest.

Margaret's teaching load was never light. Besides teaching her face-to-face classes, she also taught students online. In early March she writes, "I have put an entire course on the Internet! (Short story, in case you are wondering.) I think it may be all right. We'll see when it is piloted in the summer." Along with a course on drama, she had put courses online to benefit graduating seniors who might have been just a few hours short in earning their diplomas; so Margaret accommodated the students and the administration with her extra work. She was not complaining—she thrived on work, but later in the year she felt burdened: "I have much to discuss with you, but it needs to wait ten days. By that time the semester will be on its last legs. Me too! I wound up teaching 6 (six) regular courses this semester PLUS an independent study." She tells me in early July: "No book is worth insomnia. So what if we take a few more months. ... Give this a rest if you need to. Don't burn out! Ranulph would not approve." Margaret was considerate of others before herself, and instilled in me her passion for her beloved Ranulph—always her name for our author instead of "Higden."

For Margaret as a translator, each word was important. In late August she writes:

> The translation is still in need of "love." Let me illustrate how a Latin sequence might be made readable and significant. The phrase "canum sectatores" means literally, "associates of dogs," as you well know. You have improved to "associates of evil persons," which might be OK were it not in tandem with "diurnal drinkers" and "nocturnal sinners"—neither of which is as strong in translation as Ranulph is in the Latin. So, what did our man mean to condemn (in twenty-first century English)? ... The sequence "drunkards, robbers, scoundrels," etc., has punch to it and seems to capture the essence of Ranulph's distress.

She is ever the good teacher and goes through this sequence step by step so as not to force her opinion upon me as much as to convince me of her reasoning and encourage me to emulate her style as we work on texts and translations together. She continues:

I'm not trying to say that this is a perfect translation (in fact, I think something stronger than "scoundrel" is called for), but it tightens and strengthens the text's accusations.

The ever optimistic and confident Margaret could become overwhelmed. On December 22, she writes about the English translation that I had supplied with the Latin text:

> You've noticed, I'm sure, that I've not been forthcoming (as they say in England) about the *Speculum*. That's because I've been spending about 20 hours per chapter on the translation. There's no easy way to say this, so I'll just be blunt: it's not idiomatic and will not be understood by a modern audience. Periodically (not often) it's just plain wrong. What to do? I can continue slogging away. It will take me all of next semester at the least. I know you can revise this thing as well, but your schedule doesn't look good at all. (I should NEVER have six courses again. I have complained to the world!) … So, now you know the truth, the whole truth …. Tell me your thoughts when you have a chance.

Margaret began the year 2004 snowbound and ended the year translation-bound. I continued to supply her with revisions of my translations, which she eventually considered merely intermediate steps to her own thoughtful and engaging rendering of Ranulph's anecdotes, designed to keep the interest of the reader focused on the subject of the commandments.

Margaret Jennings: Snippets from Tutivillus's Sack

By Michael Haren

I would like to say that I met Margaret over a book. It would be an appropriate beginning to a relationship that revolved mainly (not quite exclusively) round literary discussion. And it would almost be true. It is not, though, how Margaret herself recounted the matter, and I think it right to defer to her in this. As far as she was concerned, we met over a window—an open window, channelling a stream of what I stoutly maintain to have been refreshing Oxford air. I was, indeed, mightily surprised that Margaret remembered the circumstance at all, which, until I heard her rehearse it, I had quite suppressed—in favor of the book. The book was perhaps more advantageous to me than the window, so I suppose my recollection followed the normal tendency of partiality.

The occasion of the reminiscence on her part was her introducing me to the faculty seminar that she organized on pastoral manuals at Boston College. She recalled that in the autumn of 1969 she had been sitting at H24 (or was it—the significance will emerge—H26?) in Duke Humfrey's library, when someone inexplicably set himself the objective of freezing her to death. There was a sufficient basis of fact, even if evidently misconstrued, for she had hardly begun when I caught her drift, the scene returning to me in Proustian fashion. I knew at once that this was a mismatch in the genre of Tamasin Cole's "Fourteen Rats and a Rat-Catcher," one of our children's favorite stories. (I hope that it has crossed the Atlantic, though even so it may be known only to parents of a certain age. If Tamasin Cole is actually an American author and/or if "Fourteen Rats and a Rat-Catcher" is, as it deserves to be, an evergreen, I crave pardon for my false assumptions.) In "Fourteen Rats and a Rat-Catcher," we are first introduced to a nice old lady who lived in a cottage in the forest and whose idyllic life was ruined by her having a nasty family of rats under her floor. We are then introduced to a nice rat family who lived under the floor of a tiny cottage in the forest (they were after all what the French call *une famille nombreuse*) and whose idyllic life was ruined by their having a nasty old lady living above them. The double-take continues with a long-running tussle between the parties, resolved only by the advent of the rat-catcher, who turns out to have the brokering skills of a highly gifted trade-union negotiator. Recognizing the need to redeem myself in the eyes of the seminar, I was quick to intervene with the real counterpart to Margaret's version: I was sitting in that alcove at whichever is the seat nearer the window, trying to keep my head clear with a steady supply of oxygen, only to find that every time I went to the Selden end to check a reference, I returned to a level of heat and stale air in which, it seemed to me, no normal person could work without the risk of insidious suffocation. Since in this saga, Margaret must perforce be the nice (young) lady, there is room for me only among the rats.

Margaret would in fact be doubly cast, for she had accomplished brokering skills. She leaned across to convey, pointing towards the window, that she had just come from North America, where folks lived in an air-conditioned cocoon, and that she must beg time to acclimatize. Her face was the while wreathed in the huge smile that commanded instant accommodation. She followed the information up by a no less direct observation that, whatever etiquette might be in England, she could not sit in the alcove any longer without asking to what purpose I was reading John Bromyard's *Summa predicantium* (as indeed I was, in Bodley's beautiful Nuremberg printing of 1485). Duke Humfrey was not a context where such exchanges were forbidden. I had long before taken note, indeed, that the more elevated one was within its scholarly society, the more audible one's conversation tended to be. Richard Hunt, who as Keeper of Western Manuscripts held sway over a major part, could frequently be heard passing excitedly down the central passage with news of the latest discovery. But Margaret and I were properly conscious of our juniority and, as an alternative to an appropriately hushed discussion, exited to continue over a cup of what in the Oxford of the time may have been disappointing coffee for a newly-arrived American.

So began a history which lasted the lifetime that is sadly ended. Manuscripts and rare books are now read in the splendid new Weston Library. Duke Humfrey's reading room has accordingly lost some of its centrality. As a place for quiet study, however, it continues endeavors that, though past indeed as far as involves the use of special collections, remain, in that happy dispensation of great scholarship, both an inspiration and a perennial resource. Those who witnessed the age of giants can in that magnificent shrine readily conjure up the shades of Beryl Smalley, fiercely intent on a Bible commentary, or Richard Southern (not yet Sir Richard but, if not, then president of St. John's, after he was called from the Chichele chair to occupy that office), in a state, on occasion, of relative dishabille—one cuff absent-mindedly undone. For me, Margaret too is among those who populate it still.

Before the days of the Internet our subsequent contact was punctuated by long intervals. (It is difficult to exaggerate the contribution that emailing makes to scholarly discussion, turning the world into a virtual college.) When Margaret was in Ireland, she never failed to alert me. Two visits in particular come to my mind. On one occasion she bought so much Waterford glass that the store made her a free gift of Le Creuset cast-iron cooking-ware. As this was deterrently heavy, my wife and I became the beneficiaries, receiving a handsome dish that always after we referred to as the "Margaret Jennings memorial dish." So it will remain, now all too poignantly; it shows every sign of outlasting us all. Margaret herself was an accomplished cook. On visits to her in Boston my wife and I were as impressed by her rendering of those lobster-like New England "shrimps" as I was by the formidably professional whisky-sours produced by her husband, Pat. (In partnership, they set exalted standards of hospitality.) The reputation of the "shrimps" had, indeed, preceded our own first visit, for our daughters had both made tours of the U.S. while still up at Oxford and, stopping off in Boston, had experienced that easy but attentive concern for the well-being of the young that I myself saw in action when she and Pat entertained their students.

Margaret's skills as a hostess were not only in relation to shrimps. I recall during a stay with her feeling the need for some caustic reading. I think that we had been discussing Ireland's enmeshment in the banking crisis. "Margaret," I said, "I need catharsis. Something really fierce." "Martial's fierce in an elegant way—and pithy—just right for this time of night," she said. "But I don't have him." My wife's quick thinking came to our aid. Within minutes she had bought online for my Kindle Craig A. Williams's splendid new edition of Book 2 of the *Epigrams*. Before going to bed I spent several contented hours in Margaret and Pat's comfortable study, lined with its lovely American-oak bookcases, purging my system. I shall never read Martial now without thinking of her. Not everyone would want to be thought of with Martial. I know that Margaret's free-wheelingly radical mind would relish the conjunction.

The other episode that I recall vividly from Margaret's Irish visits concerns Leonard Boyle. His tenure as prefect of the *Biblioteca Apostolica Vaticana* had just ended. I had met him in Dublin and in the aftermath I spoke to Margaret, who had known him well for about as long as I had. We formed the view that a good place for Leonard would be Blackfriars in Oxford, from where he might make a priority of resuming the work on William of Pagula, which remains, inconveniently for the many who would benefit from ready availability, still unpublished in its main bulk. (We each fell within that constituency.) The question was not really who should bell the cat. That was obvious. Such a matter required feminine skills. It was, rather, how to get the cat positioned and receptive. Margaret was in the west of Ireland, and the most convenient meeting point was Tralee, where Leonard had relations and to where he had resort for a few weeks every summer—just about the time of the Rose of Tralee festival. Before he went down to Kerry from Dublin, I told Leonard that Margaret was around, wanted to see him, and would make contact. His acute powers of divination were undiminished. He knew that something was afoot. But Margaret was so unthreatening that he indicated without reserve that he would be available.

She went to Tralee, got the message across over lunch, and reported that he was considering it seriously. *Dis aliter visum.* As became apparent soon, Leonard was not long for the world.

Siegfried Wenzel has introduced Tutivillus—a sort of snapper-up of unconsidered trifles, a puckish, marsupial version of the recording angel. Bromyard refers to him. As noted in Siegfried Wenzel's contribution, Margaret expanded massively on him. What I have inadequately assembled in response to the invitation to write a tribute to Margaret are trifles in the grand scheme, and syncopated at that. Of life as it is lived they are an essential ingredient, an indispensable element of its savor.

Reminiscences of Margaret Jennings

By Siegfried Wenzel

It must have been some day in the mid-1960s that I was sitting in my office when a young nun showed up in tears at my door, coming from the office of a colleague— a stern philologist—who obviously had not been impressed by her excitedly telling him of all the languages she wanted to learn and master, not only Latin but also biblical Greek and so forth. He had made it clear to her beyond doubt that for the direction of her graduate work she would have to look for someone else. So I got to know Margaret Jennings, then Sister Margaret. We talked about my work on sloth and the Middle Ages, and in no time Margaret had found something that interested her there: the little devil called Tutivillus who, in medieval stories, watches out for monks who in reciting the Office drop syllables, and bangs the heads of women who during Mass engage in gossip. Margaret set about checking into the passages found in my work and then discovered many more, some in Latin, others in various vernacular languages. All this she used for her Master's thesis completed in 1966, which was eventually published in an expanded form as a splendid monograph (December, 1977).

By the latter date Margaret had gone on to doctoral work, moving from Chapel Hill to Bryn Mawr, since the former did not have a certified medieval Latinist. At Bryn Mawr she worked especially on a little-known English Benedictine of the fourteenth century, Ranulph Higden. His voluminous works, most of them available only in medieval manuscripts, were to keep her busy for the rest of her days.

Our paths crossed every once in a while. Margaret would visit us briefly in Swarthmore, Pennsylvania, and even claimed she was present at the baptismal party for my youngest daughter, which happened in early 1969 in Oxford (I have no recollection of Margaret's being present, though). Oxford, because Margaret pursued medieval manuscripts with great zeal at the Bodleian as well as in other major European libraries. And to looking up manuscripts she soon added looking at medieval cathedrals, all this not simply to satisfy her own curiosity, delight, and scholarly work, but also as a background for her teaching aspects of the medieval world and its Christian culture. Our paths also crossed on home territory. There was that most memorable evening at one annual meeting of the Modern Language Association where she had entertained a number of colleagues at her house in Brooklyn, and the festivities and excellent dinner were followed by a hair-raising taxi ride back to our convention hotel.

After many such get-togethers at professional meetings we met again after several years in Boston and then especially at her lovely home in Framingham, full of antiques, and an impressive one itself, after Margaret had found renewed happiness in her marriage to Pat. There we sat and talked shop until, after two days of pretty much uninterrupted Brooklyn accent, I just had to go out and hear a Bostonian for a change. Her last years of often grueling teaching at St. Joseph's College were happily crowned by an endowed professorship at Boston College, where she could draw on her scholarship and impressions of her favorite French cathedral, that of Bourges, and where at one point I was privileged to respond to her paper dealing with her lifelong Chief Author, the Benedictine Ranulph Higden.

Eyewitness: Ranulph Higden and the Troubling Events at Chester Monastery*

By Margaret Jennings

Ranulph Higden's most significant contribution to the literature of pastoral care is a manual of instruction called the *Speculum curatorum*, a lengthy text compiled originally in 1340 and revised about 1350. The only known copy of the later recension occupies all 295 folios of Urbana-Champaign, University of Illinois, MS. Pre-1650, 72,[1] a vellum manuscript—2 cm long and 19 cm wide—written in Anglicana by several scribes.[2] The two versions identify the author through an acrostic, derived from the initial letters of consecutive chapters, that contains the words: "Cestrensis monachus Ranulphus" (Ranulph, a monk of Chester).[3]

In addition, as was the norm with other manuals in this genre, both the 1340 and 1350 texts regularly depend on John of Freiburg's *Summa confessorum* (1298); occasionally, as well, they use the *Manipulus curatorum* (1333) of Guido de Monte Rocherii, the *Oculus sacerdotis* (ca. 1320–1328) of William of Pagula, the *Summa*

---

* This essay originally appeared in *Studies in Medieval and Renaissance History*, 3rd series, vol. 7 (2010): 167–93. It is reprinted here with kind permission of AMS Press, Inc.

[1] Under the aegis of Dallas Medieval Texts, an edition/translation of the entire manuscript (by Eugene Crook and Margaret Jennings) is forthcoming from Peeters in Leuven: vol. 1 (*On the Commandments*) and vol. 2 (*On the Sins*) in early 2010 and vol. 3 (*On the Sacraments*) in 2011. [Editorial note: Both volumes 1 and 2 have since appeared; volume 3 is to follow within the next couple of years. The passages cited with folio numbers in the present article can easily be identified in the printed text, which has the folio numbers in the margins.]

[2] The manuscript has 38 gatherings of eight folios, each with a few anomalies. The eighth gathering lacks the last leaf, and there is an obvious lacuna in the text; the sixteenth has only two folios, but there is no missing material; what is wanting in later gatherings seems to be due to carelessness or to the ravages of time and usage.

[3] Eugene Crook, "A New Version of Ranulph Higden's *Speculum Curatorum*," *Manuscripta* 21 (1977): 44–7, introduces the Illinois manuscript; the article includes Neil Ker's description of the text and provides detailed information about signatures, catchword usages, and rubric variations. Crook also suggests a stemma for the manuscripts which preserve the 1340 version and compares their acrostic schemes with that of the 1350 recension.

confessorum (ca. 1302) of John of Erfurt, and assorted works of other prominent medieval authors like Augustine, Gregory the Great, Anselm, and Thomas Aquinas.[4]

The Illinois recension, however, differs markedly from the earlier version in organizational plan, length, and emphasis. A perusal of its contents, moreover, reveals that Ranulph's handling of instructional material makes reference to and seems affected by disturbing events within his own monastery: continuous and wide-ranging dissension among the monks, violent behavior in several abbots, a flagrant disregard for religious vows, especially chastity, and dissolute living prompted by gluttony.

The contrast between the two texts is immediately apparent in their development patterns. In the four British manuscripts,[5] which preserve the first version of the *Speculum*, key doctrines in the magisterium are addressed almost identically in terms of length of treatment and content. The chapters are numbered consecutively and form a continuous whole with 30 percent devoted to the deadly sins, 50 percent to the sacraments, and the rest dealing with disparate subjects like the evangelical counsels, tithes, the gifts of the Holy Spirit, the beatitudes, free will and grace, sorcery and superstition, the virtues in general and in particular, fraternal correction, and faith and love. One chapter is prefatory, and only one treats the commandments. Except for the extended discussion of the tricks of the demons, the topics handled are consistent with what Archbishop John Pecham's *De informacione simplicium sacerdotum* of 1281[6] had deemed essential to understanding Christianity: the articles of faith, the Decalogue, the vices and virtues, and the sacraments.

The 1350 text exhibits a very different organizational plan. It is divided into three books—"On the Commandments" (50 chapters, fols. 1r–63v), "On the Sins" (51 chapters, fols. 64r–114v), and "On the Sacraments" (109 chapters, fols. 115r–295v)—a triplicate structure which may have been suggested by the triplex patterning of the prescriptive and popular *artes praedicandi*.[7] In its exposition, it

---

[4] See Leonard E. Boyle, "The *Summa Confessorum* of John of Freiburg and the Popularization of the Moral Teaching of St. Thomas and Some of His Contemporaries," in *Pastoral Care, Clerical Education and Canon Law* (London, 1981), 2:248–58.

[5] Durham, Dean and Chapter Library, MS. B.iv.36; Cambridge, University Library, MS. Mn i.20; London, British Library, MS. Harley 1004; Oxford, Balliol College, MS. 77. These manuscripts are described respectively in T. Rud and J. Rayne, *Codicum Manuscriptorum Ecclesiae Cathedralis Dunelmensis* (Durham, 1825), 241; *A Catalogue of the Manuscripts Preserved in the Library of the University of Cambridge* (New York, 1980), 4:115; *A Catalogue of the Harleian Manuscripts in the British Museum* (London, 1808), 1:502b; and R. A. B. Mynors, *Catalogue of the Manuscripts of Balliol College, Oxford* (Oxford, 1963), 62.

[6] F. M. Powicke and C. R. Cheney (eds.), *Councils & Synods with Other Documents Relating to the English Church* (Oxford, 1964), 2.2:900–05.

[7] Margaret Jennings and Sally A. Wilson (trans.), *Ranulph Higden, Ars componendi sermones* (Leuven, 2003), 43–4.

seems to embrace the catechetical program set forth in Robert Grosseteste's *Templum domini*, where the commandments are the primary subject for development, followed by the sins and the sacraments.[8] The most notable expansion in the 1350 edition is Ranulph's explanation of and commentary on the Decalogue, which now commands a whole book of 50 chapters. Other expansions are occasioned by the manner in which important topics are treated. For example, each deadly sin is defined and then further subdivided into its various species, its daughters (or sins that arise from it), and its remedies (either an opposed virtue or a remedial action).[9] The ramifications of all sins are carefully discussed in separate chapters; as a result, in the 1350 edition, the incentives for, incitements to, and damages of lust merit eleven chapters, not one and a half; gluttony is detailed in seven, not two, chapters. The sacraments still occupy about 50 percent of the text, but penance is no longer paramount.[10] Even though Ranulph decides to omit a large portion of his 1340 Speculum in 1350—almost half of the material, according to the editor—the revision is about 28 percent longer overall.[11]

The differences in organization and length presage other changes in emphasis. The 1340 text focused on the lacunae in priestly education as Higden perceived them because "the office of the priest is chiefly concerned with two things ... the instruction of those subordinate to him and the ministry of the sacraments."[12] It is possible that a few of those priest-pastors may also have been monks, but Ranulph does not discuss this possibility and maintains a teaching stance throughout. In the 1350 edition, though, the instructional material does not aim to assist the priest in his twofold role, but rather to illumine the three things absolutely imposed on every living Christian in order to achieve salvation—namely, observing the Decalogue, avoiding sin, and embracing the sacramental system; indeed, pastors must devote themselves to promoting these three activities "as their most important duty."[13] Additional

---

[8] Powicke and Cheney, *Councils*, 2.1:268.

[9] Ranulph's treatment of envy—with appropriate variations—is reiterated for each sin; see Urbana-Champaign, University of Illinois, MS Pre-1650, 72, fols. 77v–81r: "De inuidia," "De filiabus inuidie," "De detraccione," and "De remedio inuidie."

[10] In 1350, penance occupied one quarter of the sacramental discussion; in 1340, it had claimed almost a third of the discussion.

[11] Eugene Crook has been studying what is omitted and, in a private communication to me, made this calculation.

[12] Translated in Crook, "New Version," 44–5.

[13] Ranulph's phrase is "summo opere." For the complete context, see Urbana-Champaign, University of Illinois, MS. Pre-1650, 72, fol. 1r: "Cum a saluatore tria potissime cuilibet christiano hic dum viuerit sint indicta obseruare videlicet mandata dominica, deuitare delicta mortifica, et participare sacramenta saluifica, summo opere curandum est ipsis plebium rectoribus ... vt habeant noticiam in hiis tribus ...." Unless otherwise noted, all Latin quotations are taken from this manuscript.

impetus toward this end arises from the fact that the mid-fourteenth century is a time of multiple and despicable abuses when "pagan worship rises next to the altar, the gold [of God's kingdom] is tarnished, the stones of the sanctuary are scattered, the flock walks along dangerous paths, the wolf mangles at will, the sheepfold of Christ is trampled underfoot."[14] The urgency conveyed by the preface is reflected in the text, where Ranulph seems driven not only to expand his discussion but also to specify, exemplify, and codify.[15] Within this process, he also allows his readers to glimpse the perilous state of the once mighty monastic institution to which he had devoted his life.

For the four centuries prior to Higden's commencing his religious life there, the foundation at Chester had been developing steadily in size, prestige, and prosperity. At that location, in tandem with the tenth-century Scandinavian settlements that accelerated the rise of a new English elite,[16] a religious house had been established about 907, probably for secular clerics. From 1092 to 1093, Hugh, earl of Chester, "expelled the seculars and, with Anselm's help, Benedictines were introduced from Bec-Hellouin."[17] The monastery, dedicated to St. Werburgh—best known and loved of the Saxon saints—gradually became one of the most powerful religious houses in England and, by 1249, the number of monks had increased to forty.[18] Although the abbey's reputation fluctuated at a few points in the early to mid-thirteenth century, its reputation and finances were secured under the extensive and productive abbacies

---

[14] Fol. 1r: "quod videlicet lucus crescit iuxta altare, quod obscuratum est aurum, quod dispersi sunt lapides sanctuarii, quod grex graditur per abrupta, quod lupus lacerat, quod caula Christi conculcatur."

[15] For example, in fol. 31r (1340 version) of Durham, Dean and Chapter Library MS. B.iv.36, the chapter "De fraterna correpcione" begins: "Ut plenius pateat de correpcione fraterna, notandum est secundum Thomam in Summa quod ista correpcio cadit sub precepto" ("In order that fraternal correction may be more plainly explicated, it is to be noted, according to Thomas in the *Summa*, that such correction is enjoined by precept"). In the 1350 edition, and consistently throughout this text, the subject to be treated is clearly defined, almost anxiously divided, and then explained and illustrated. Emblematic of this methodology is the first book's chapter 49, on the same subject, "De consilio fraterne correpcionis" (fol. 59v), which starts with a summary statement: "Christi zelum habere videtur qui fratrem corripit" ("He who corrects his brother seems to possess the zeal of Christ") and then sets up the procedure to be followed: "circa quod queritur primo, quid sit correpcio; secundo, an cadat sub precepto; tercio, an ad omnes extendatur" ("about this subject is asked first, what correction is; second, whether it is enjoined by precept; third, whether it is extended to all"), and so forth to a thirteenth topic for discussion.

[16] Data supplied by T. Austin and cited in John Bradley, "A Tale of Three Cities," in *Ireland, England, and the Continent*, ed. H. Clarke and J. R. S. Phillips (Dublin, 2006), 51–66, here 54.

[17] David Knowles and R. Neville Hadcock, *Medieval Religious Houses: England and Wales* (London, 1971), 62, and J. C. Dickinson, *Monastic Life in Medieval England* (London, 1961), 69.

[18] From the Victoria History of the Counties of England: *A History of the County of Chester*, vol. 3, ed. B. E. Harris (Oxford, 1980), 138.

of Simon Whitchurch (1265–1291) and his successor, Thomas Birchills (1291–1323).[19]

The era of prosperity and good order at Chester's monastery (ca. 1270–1330) coincided with a period in which English Benedictine life was definitively altered as a series of reform statutes effectuated a wide-ranging overhaul of the diverse customs practiced in the now numerous foundations.[20] Between 1277 and 1336, dietary restrictions, requirements for the holding of offices and personal property, and understandings about geographical mobility were regularized; the obligations to extensive periods of prayer and other disciplinary practices were modified; chapter meetings were organized and legislated, as were educational initiatives, particularly at the university level.[21] Papal support for these alterations, which created a centralized, unified governance system, is evident in the canons of "Summi magistri," issued by Pope Benedict XII on June 20, 1336.[22]

For forty of the sixty years during which the reforms were being implemented, Ranulph Higden embraced Benedictine life at Chester and embodied the monastic ideal of "ora et labora." The colophon in a copy of the *Polychronicon* (now Oxford, Bodleian Library, MS. Laud Misc. 619) and a note on the flyleaf of another *Polychronicon* copy (now Oxford, New College Library, MS. 162) indicate that he entered St. Werburgh's in 1299 and died there either in 1363 or 1364, possibly on the feast of St. Gregory.[23] There is no evidence that he attended university, although several of his brother monks were sent to study at Gloucester College, Oxford, by order of the provincial chapter.[24] According to an entry on the close roll for August, 1352, he was summoned on the eighth of that month to King Edward III's presence "cum omnibus chronicis vestris," a summons that must have been both honorific and onerous since he was probably nearing seventy—long beyond the life expectancy

---

[19] From the Victoria History of the Counties of England: *A History of the County of Chester*, vol. 5, ed. C. P. Lewis and A. T. Thacker (Woodbridge, 2003), 80. Hereafter cited as *VCH Ches.* with the volume number and page. Although some abuses occurred at Chester during this period, there was no great outcry; see R. V. H. Burne, *The Monks of Chester* (London, 1962), 66–70.

[20] David Knowles surveys the compelling reasons for change in *The Religious Orders in England*, vol. 1 (Cambridge, 1955), 9–21.

[21] James G. Clark, "Introduction," in *The Religious Orders in Pre-Reformation England*, ed. idem (Woodbridge, 2002), 11–12.

[22] Knowles, *Religious Orders*, vol. 2, p. 3.

[23] Gregory's feast day is March 12. See John Taylor, *The Universal Chronicle of Ranulph Higden* (Oxford, 1966), 1–2.

[24] William A. Pantin, *Documents Illustrating the Activities of the General and Provincial Chapters of the English Black Monks, 1215–1540*, vol. 2 (Cambridge, 1933), 16–17; John Taylor, "Higden, Ranulf (d. 1364)," *Oxford Dictionary of National Biography*, vol. 27 (Oxford, 2004), 49–50.

of his era.[25] The few records from St. Werburgh's that survived the Dissolution indicate that he took no part in the internal strife that troubled the abbey during the latter part of his life, a situation in keeping with his position as monk-scholar and probable head of the scriptorium.[26]

That Higden deserves the sobriquet "monk-scholar" is attested by several works, the most well-known being his *Polychronicon*, a lengthy text designed to give the learned people of fourteenth-century England a new perspective on their world.[27] Its roots and general subject matter were in the medieval tradition of the universal chronicle, but Higden added his antiquarian interests and the early history of Britain to the mix. Finished originally in 1327, continued to 1340, and worked over for several years afterward, the *Polychronicon*, by its scope, completeness, and wide-ranging references, types Higden as an "encyclopedist" rather than as a "historian proper."[28] This chronicle's obvious thoroughness may explain its pre-Reformation popularity; it is estimated that hundreds of copies existed in the early sixteenth century.[29] A similar orientation to comprehensive coverage of topics is discernible in other works attributed to Higden: an *Ars kalendarii*, *Distinctiones theologicae*, a *Pedagogium artis grammaticae*, and an *Abbreviationes chronicorum*.[30] But the monk's place in the history of the later medieval church—and in modern scholarship about the pastoral renewal that vastly affected it—is owed in small part to his *Ars componendi sermones* but, chiefly, to his *Speculum curatorum*. Higden's *Ars componendi sermones* is a well-crafted, clearly explained prescriptive treatise about how compositional structures—analogous

---

[25] Because of the Black Death, it is difficult to determine life expectancy in the mid-fourteenth century. A recent study, which commences at the year 1395, indicates that monks in geographically separated monasteries had approximately the same life expectancy: under 50 years. See John Hatcher, A. J. Piper, and David Stone, "Monastic Mortality: Durham Priory, 1395–1529," *Economic History Review* 59 (2006): 667–87.

[26] Margaret Jennings, "Higden's Minor Writings and the Fourteenth-Century Church," *Proceedings of the Leeds Philosophical and Literary Society* 16 (1977): 149–58, here 151.

[27] Ibid. and Taylor, *Universal Chronicle*, 2. The breadth of Higden's achievement is also demonstrated in Chris Given-Wilson, *Chronicles: The Writing of History in Medieval England* (London, 2004), esp. 55–9, 113–19, and 130–4.

[28] V. H. Galbraith, "An Autograph MS. of Ranulph Higden's *Polychronicon*," *Huntington Library Quarterly* 23 (1959): 1–18, here 17.

[29] Jennings, "Minor Writings," 151.

[30] Both secular and Benedictine bibliographers attribute these works to Higden; no dates, however, are assigned. The *Ars kalendarii* and the *Abbreviationes* are very likely his and, because of their use in other works, they must have been completed before 1340. Higden may have written the *Distinctiones* and the *Pedagogium*, but it is not possible to confirm this. His putative authorship of the Chester plays has long been discredited as the plays date to the mid-fifteenth century at the earliest; see Theresa Coletti, "The Chester Cycle in Sixteenth-Century Religious Culture," *Journal of Medieval and Early Modern Studies* 37 (2007): 531–47, here 531. Taylor, *Universal Chronicle*, 182–4, surveys all viable attributions.

to those in Ciceronian *dispositio*—can be used to mold a "modern" sermon.[31] Aside from its author's dislike of playacting, few references to contemporary conditions can be found in the *Ars*.[32] Nevertheless, the text occupies a unique place in the history of *pastoralia* since Ranulph is the only Benedictine monk to have written an *ars praedicandi*.

In contrast to the *Ars*, the 1350 version of the *Speculum curatorum* bears important witness to the changing monastic situation in which Higden lived. Either simultaneously with or immediately after the publication of the *Speculum*'s earlier edition, a series of troubling incidents began at St. Werburgh's. Burne offers collateral reasons for these distresses: with a poetic flourish he traces the lowering of religious standards at the abbey to the fact that the age of faith was giving place to the age of chivalry; with a practical eye he sees that this supplanting was exacerbated by the reality of the Hundred Years War.[33] Whether their explanation be practical or poetic, the disturbing events were both continuous and noteworthy. In 1340, for instance, the abbot seized most of the assets of Chipping Camden in Gloucestershire. In itself, this was not very alarming since, on previous occasions, he had appropriated livings whenever there was a financial difficulty; this time, however, the income was assigned to the cellarer.[34] This hint of sumptuousness in the refectory and, by extension, of laxity in discipline was writ large a few years later in the twenty-first year of William Bebington's abbacy. Probably to avoid interference from the conscientious Bishop Roger Northburgh and his officials, the abbot, in 1345, sought certain exemptions from episcopal control without securing either the consent of the monks or of the abbey's patron, the Black Prince.[35] As this action followed by just a year his acquisition of a papal license to exercise episcopal and archidiaconal jurisdiction over his servants and the parishioners of the abbey's altar of St. Oswald,[36] there was immediate opposition from four senior members of the community. Unable to appeal to the oversight of the local ordinary, the monks appealed to the royal house.[37] In 1346, Bebington, now unequivocally accused of "dissolute living," was summoned to court,

---

[31] See the Introduction to the *Ars* in Jennings and Wilson, *Higden, Ars*, 1–8.

[32] The clause "nec ad sui ostentacionem sicut faciunt olei venditores" ("nor for self-ostentation as with oil vendors") probably refers to the oil vendor segment in a Resurrection play. Chester's Whitsun plays—in a nascent condition in Ranulph's lifetime—were staged in front of the abbey and the commotion they caused possibly interfered with Higden's scholarship. See Margaret Jennings, *The Ars componendi sermones of Ranulph Higden, O.S.B.* (Leiden, 1991), 7 and Jennings and Wilson, *Higden, Ars*, 71 n. 6.

[33] Burne, *Monks of Chester*, 77.

[34] Ibid., 80.

[35] Ibid., 79.

[36] *VCH Ches.* 3:139.

[37] Burne, *Monks of Chester*, 79.

and the monks who had brought the charges were given refuge outside of Chester.[38] Nevertheless, except for some ineffectual hand-wringing, the problem remained unaddressed. In 1348, Abbot William obtained papal protection from deposition.[39] With the abbot now practically untouchable, bitterness, internal faction, and misrule became the order of the day. Upon the death of Bebington, who probably succumbed to plague in November, 1349,[40] many of the monks must have hoped that this distressing period would cease.

Unfortunately, the abbey's decline continued unabated under the subsequent abbacy of Richard Seynesbury (1349–1362), who "was a man of violence and whose example was followed by at least some of his monks."[41] Exactly how a person of such questionable character could have been elected is unfathomable; there may be a clue in the first book of the 1350 edition of the *Speculum*, chapter 35, where Higden mentions the vitiating effect of fear on monastic elections.[42] What is known of the consequent lawlessness at the monastery must have distressed the monk-scholar. Burne recounts that within months of his ascendancy, Seynesbury was

> set upon by a party of his own monks and severely beaten, while his two companions … were wounded. The perpetrators of this outrage were William Merston and William Peck, monks of the said abbey, John Grey, clerk, and Henry de Kelsall, acting with the assent and counsel of two other monks.[43]

The inconsequential legal proceedings following upon this incident did nothing to resolve the tension; nor did accusations in 1350 and several subsequent years that the abbot had ordered various depredations in the countryside.[44]

It seems indisputable that the 1350 edition of the *Speculum* was promulgated at a time of considerable upheaval within Chester monastery. Additionally, no one, not even a Ranulph Higden who had had to contend with a great decline in the discipline exercised and the virtue practiced among the monks, could have imagined the cataclysmic effect on the clerical population of the bubonic plague outbreak in 1348 and 1349. Current estimations place the death toll on the English clergy at 70 percent.[45] Although Chester itself may not have experienced so disastrously high a death

---

[38] *VCH Ches.* 3:139.

[39] Burne, *Monks of Chester*, 80.

[40] Philip Ziegler, *The Black Death* (New York, 1969), 189.

[41] Burne, *Monks of Chester*, 84.

[42] Fol. 43v: "in eleccionibus excusat et viciat" ("in elections, it vitiates and voids").

[43] Burne, *Monks of Chester*, 84–5.

[44] Ibid., 85. See also *VCH Ches.* 3, 140.

[45] John Aberth, *The Black Death: The Great Mortality of 1348–1350* (New York, 2005), 125. Cf. William J. Dohar, *The Black Death and Pastoral Leadership* (Philadelphia, 1995).

rate, it cannot have escaped the bacterial scourge. With many priests and a considerably smaller group of monks[46] unprepared for assuming the parochial duties suddenly thrust upon them, manuals like the *Speculum* played a critical role. Parish clergy—mediators between God and his people—were literally and figuratively to be "doctors skilled by practice,"[47] as they handled numerous sociological and psychological crises as well as parochial desiderata. Like most of his contemporaries who were without images or vocabulary to convey the horror they had experienced,[48] Ranulph does not specifically discuss the miseries of the Black Death. Its effects, however, may linger in the way the *Speculum* was altered. Unfortunately, the attractive, and perhaps viable, hypothesis that all the changes made in the Illinois text resulted from the Black Death cannot be confirmed. It is possible, however, to demonstrate what happened to specific content areas in the later edition: paragraphs were reordered, sentences shortened or formulated more precisely, and vocabulary explained to achieve an untrammeled communication of ideas.[49] Since Ranulph's 1350 audience was faced with multiple and staggering problems, it seems that a patently clear structure and an immediately comprehensible discussion of commandments, sins, and sacraments were now of major importance.

Moreover, the emphasis in the 1350 recension on each person's responsibility in developing God's kingdom allowed Ranulph to look harshly on the religious situation of post-plague Chester, and especially at St. Werburgh's monastery, rife as it was with violations of standard moral teaching on social relations and individual conduct. His opening critique, in *Speculum*, Book I, chapter 1, points a finger at the clerical population in general; the fact that by this time at least two of his brother monks were engaged in the *cura animarum* makes the indictment more stinging. Higden shapes his discussion according to the traditional roles that clergy were to

---

[46] Cuthbert Butler, in *Benedictine Monachism* (London, 1924), 417, claims that quite a few monks had the *cura animarum* thrust upon them; recorded cases are, however, not many, although, at St. Werburgh's, monks served the parish altar of St. Oswald in 1349 and the parish of Weston-on-Trent, which was in the abbey's patrimony. See Burne, *Monks of Chester*, 91 and Jennings, "Minor Writings," 150.

[47] The phrase "more periti medici" was commonplace as a result of its use in the 21st canon ("Omnis utriusque sexus") promulgated by the Fourth Lateran Council in 1215; see *Conciliorum oecumenicorum decreta*, ed. Centro di documentazione, Istituto per le scienze religiose, Bologna, curantibus Josepho Alberigo et al. (Freiburg, 1962), 321.

[48] John B. Friedman, "'He hath a thousand slayn this pestilence': The Iconography of the Plague in the Later Middle Ages," in *Social Unrest in the Late Middle Ages*, ed. Francis X. Newman (Binghamton, 1986), 75–112, here 75.

[49] Ranulph's editorial practice is studied in Eugene Crook and Margaret Jennings, "The Devil and Ranulph Higden," *Manuscripta* 22 (1978): 131–40, here 136–8.

assume in the care of souls: shepherd, watchman, mediator.[50] In the aftermath of
the Black Death,

> [t]he leader—confused through lack of knowledge—cannot discern how he may safely
> lead the flock. … The watchman lulled to sleep through impurity—cannot keep awake
> in order to beware of perils. … The mediator—distracted by discontent and absence—will
> not be able to conciliate in order to banish wrath.[51]

This harsh critique, which appears only in the 1350 edition, continues as Ranulph
explores the three causes for failure mentioned above. It is his conviction that ignorance inflicts the most damage because it renders instruction impossible and disables
the volitional faculty;[52] through it, pastors themselves fall into excess and unclean-
ness and become "gamblers, cheats, drunkards, and perverts."[53]

> Proceeding from such irregularities, a fourth abuse easily develops, namely: although the
> aforesaid curates do not take care as leaders, they are not on guard as watchmen and do
> not reconcile as mediators. Nevertheless, they exact wages and gather stipends just like the
> diligent workers of the Lord's vineyard.[54]

In addition to fraud and avarice, Ranulph imputes to the clergy many other fail-
ings, styling them "worthy of as many modes of death as they gave examples of death
to their followers."[55] Having done considerable harm to the present and future

---

[50] These activities, often conjoined with the act of preaching, are cited by several later medieval preach-
ers. See Siegfried Wenzel, *Latin Sermon Collections from Later Medieval England* (Cambridge, 2005),
269.

[51] Fol. 1r: "Set reuera ductor excecatus per ignoranciam videre non potest vt gregem sane ducat. …
Item speculator soporatus per immundiciam vigilare non potest vt pericula precaueat. … Mediator
quoque elongatus per displicenciam et absenciam placare non poterit vt iram ammoueat." The 1340
version does not contain any comparable critique of clerical malfeasance, nor does it directly accuse
religious groups—regular or secular—of breaches in discipline or failure to provide good example. All
comments of this nature appear in the 1350 text; most are discussed below.

[52] Fol. 1r: "nec se nec alios nouit instruere" ("he knows how to instruct neither himself nor others")
and "vt intellectiua pastoris per ignoranciam excecata, affectiua siue operatiua facilius seducatur" ("as
the intellectual faculty of the pastor is disabled through ignorance, the volitional or operative faculty is
more easily led astray").

[53] The literal translation of fol. 1r: "alee lusores, canum sectatores, diurni potatores, nocturni pecca-
tores" is "players of dice, followers of dogs, drinkers by day, sinners by night." Abuses mentioned later
in the text suggest the words "cheats" and "perverts" for the second and fourth designations, which are
otherwise meaningless.

[54] Fol. 1v: "facile quartum sequitur abusiuum quod scilicet cum predicti curati non videant vt ductores,
non vigilent vt speculatores, non reconcilient vt mediatores. Mercedem tamen exigunt et stipendia
percipiunt, tanquam Dominice vinee seduli excultores."

[55] Fol. 1r: "vt iam tot mortibus digni sint, quot mortis exempla ad suos subditos transmiserunt."

church, "finally, the pastor thus defiled and seduced by his own concupiscence is removed."[56]

Without doubt, Higden's harangue is primarily directed to secular clergy and only peripherally to monks. The latter, however, were the target group for his often cutting discourse—unique to the 1350 text—on apostate religious, the vowed life, obedience and disobedience as practiced in monastic precincts, relationships of regular clergy with authority, and scandal as a particular danger in community living.[57]

He identifies the third type of apostasy—the withdrawal from clerical life or from a religious order of a person who had vowed commitment to that life or order—as an "irregularity."[58] Like the word "prelatus," which was applied somewhat indiscriminately to authority figures both inside and outside the church, there are multiple definitions for "irregularis" in the fourteenth century; the word's meaning ranges from periodic, unsanctioned absence to absconding completely; it can signify anywhere along the continuum from unusual to criminal behavior; it may designate neglect of a religious rule or flagrant disregard of that rule. In the context of this sixteenth chapter of the *Speculum*, Book I, "irregular apostasy" means absconding completely from the clerical state or from one's convent or monastery. St. Werburgh's had suffered few (if any) apostasies prior to 1350,[59] a fact that might explain Ranulph's casualness in making what sound like rote recommendations to apostates who are refused re-entrance into their former religious houses;[60] the same air of insouciance probably accounts for his failure to enumerate apostasy's spiritual consequences. Rather, his discussion focuses on its financial implications, an emphasis which could reflect the monetary uncertainties at the monastery as its relationship

---

[56] Fol. 1r: "Tandem pastor sic pollutus a propria concupiscencia illectus abstrahitur."

[57] In the 1350 *Speculum*, apostate religious are discussed in chapter 16 under the umbrella of the first commandment; the vowed life and obedience/disobedience in chapter 21 under the umbrella of the second commandment and in Book II, chapters 10 and 11 (about the "Daughters of Pride" and the "Degrees of Pride"); relationships with authority are mentioned in several places, especially as a prelude to the topic of scandal in chapters 28 and 29 under the umbrella of the fifth commandment. Scandal also appears briefly in the 1340 text, appended to a discussion of "Sin in Particular" in chapter 19; in 1350, however, it occupies a separate chapter of almost two complete folios (39v–41r).

[58] Fol. 20r: "Irregularitatis quando quis recedit sponte ab ordine clericali conuersando vt laicus vel quando quis recedit a religione quam professus est ad seculum."

[59] No apostasies prior to 1350 are listed in F. Donald Logan, *Runaway Religious in Medieval England: 1240–1540* (Cambridge, 1996).

[60] Fol. 30r: "Tales debent facere obedienciam alieno prelato, et de eorum licencia vti rebus suis elemosinam dare; vestem religiosam deferant, horas canonicas dicant, ieiunia seruent." ("Such persons ought to render obedience to another superior and, with the [appropriate] permission, use their goods to give alms; let them wear religious clothing, say the canonical hours, and preserve fasts.")

with and donations from the surrounding area declined.[61] Ranulph states that whatever a returning apostate acquired in the secular world devolves to his monastery; nevertheless, he is equally clear—and fair—in stating that if the apostate is permitted to go to a more difficult rule, then his acquired goods devolve to the second monastery.[62] Apostasy precludes the acts of virtue conterminous with observing the vows of poverty, chastity, and obedience discussed in chapter twenty-one.[63] And, when the vowed life is denigrated, collateral abuses can occur. This realization may have prompted Higden to oppose the ideal of living virtuously with what he sees in his contemporaries: "living voluptuously."[64] He is dismayed that a prospective postulant, after viewing such reprehensible behavior, thinks "that he could maintain [such a lifestyle] and so joins that group."[65] That some voluptuous activity occurred within or near the precincts of St. Werburgh's is suggested by the *Speculum*'s several references to monks who engaged in fornication[66] and to the fact that legal proceedings against Richard of Chester were instituted in 1356 by Thomas de Bredon and "Joan, his wife"; the Thomas de Bredon mentioned here is conceivably the same person who was a monk of Chester and sometime pastor of the abbey's church at Weston-on-Trent.[67]

Most telling is Ranulph's discussion of sacrilegious fornication in the 1350 *Speculum*'s Book II, chapter 47. The tone of this denunciation is abrasive—very different from his grousings about a self-centered individual who, in order to seem holy, "clears his throat, coughs, moans, and fills with sighs the ears of anyone tarrying outside his choir stall."[68] In this final chapter on lust, Ranulph states unequivocally that for many clerics, the "crown" is not manifest nor tonsure appropriate.[69] This sentence's use of

---

[61] A growing indifference between the town and the abbey meant that few citizens chose to be buried or commemorated there, resulting in a dearth of monies from that source; see *VCH Ches.* 5, 81.

[62] Fol. 20r: "quicquid apostata adquirit in seculo cedit monasterio suo" ("whatever the apostate acquired in the secular world devolves to his monastery") and "adquirat [fol. 20v] aliqua bona illa cedunt monasterio secundo" ("should he acquire any goods, these devolve to the second monastery").

[63] Vows as acts of virtue are mentioned several times; the most specific mention is that on fol. 26r: "… votum proprie est de meliori bono … quod pertinet ad actum virtutis" ("… a vow properly speaking is about a higher good … which pertains to an act of virtue").

[64] Fol. 27v: "viuere molliter."

[65] Fol. 27v: "quod hec posset sustinere et sic intrat."

[66] Fornication as a clerical abuse is also treated in chapters five, twenty-nine, and fifty of Book I of the *Speculum*.

[67] See Jennings, "Minor Writings," 155 n. 12 and Burne, *Monks of Chester*, 85–6.

[68] Fol. 75v: "… screat, tussit, gemit, aures extramanencium de angulo suo suspiris replet."

[69] Fol. 111r: "dico nec est corona patens nec tonsura conveniens." Ranulph could be playing with "corona" (crown of the head) as a synonym for tonsure, but he may also be using the word "crown" to symbolize the physical state of virginity, as occurs in *The Pearl*.

"tonsure" and the later reference to "habitations of clerics" would seem to include in Ranulph's indictment not only the Benedictines, but also the Dominicans, Franciscans, and Carmelites—all of whom had installations in medieval Chester.[70] However, the distance of these convents from St. Werburgh's, the very specific nature of the accusations, Ranulph's age (probably nearing seventy), and his vow of stability tend to confirm that his brother monks have occasioned his angry words:

> In clothing they are wanton, in gesture insolent, in words filthy, in divine offices negligent; and they come together mostly to amuse themselves and to mock and ridicule. They rush to revels and drinking bouts, so much so that today the habitations of clerics are considered the bordellos of prostitutes, a place for engaging in gambling, incantations, and wild dancing. Even in the middle of the night there is shouting and drinking. Thus, what rightly belongs to the poor is expended prodigally, banquets are set forth with great extravagance, birds and dogs are impiously procured from the property of the church. With regard to these actions, the people cry out and the congregation murmurs while the bishops cover them up and superiors make light of them.[71]

The context and content of the "shouting" seems to be specified by the disrespectful modes of behavior and word parodies detailed in the later recension of the *Speculum*, Book II, chapter 36: "How Difficult It Is to Overcome Gluttony." Ranulph's usage resembles the parodies associated with the "Spielermesse";[72] his locale is clearly the cloister as chanting the Hours of the Divine Office and preparing for the liturgy are the actions indicated—the former through the words "readings," "responsories," and "psalms" and the latter by "procession," "chalice," and "Dominus vobiscum," the most common greeting of the Mass. All, however, are corrupted and so, instead of following a horarium structured by liturgical actions, the gluttonous monks observe a very different lifestyle:

> In place of calls to prayer are invitations to drinking, in place of readings are tales of the wicked, in place of responsories are words of wariness, in place of psalms are flattery and lies, in place of genuflections are swearings on the knees to continue drinking, in place of

---

[70] See J. Patrick Greene, *Medieval Monasteries* (Leicester, 1992), 163 and Joseph Turmel, André Lagarde, and Archibald Alexander, *The Latin Church in the Middle Ages*, trans. Archibald Alexander (New York, 1915), 83–125.

[71] Fol. 111r: "set in veste lasciuia, in gestu insolencia, in verbis immundicia, in diuinis officiis necligencia, magis ad ludendum, ad ridendum, ad deridendum congregati. Currunt ad commessaciones, ad ebrietates vt, iam, habitacula clericorum plus putentur prostibula meretricum, in quibus versantur alearum iactus, cantus, et saltus. Vsque ad mediam noctem clamatur et potatur. Sic, bona pauperum expenduntur prodige conuiuia perantur [sic] splendide, aues et canes de bonis ecclesie procurantur impie. Hoc, populus clamat, plebs submurmurat, dissimulant episcopi, necligunt prelati."

[72] Martha Bayless, *Parody in the Middle Ages* (Ann Arbor, 1996), 99–123.

the procession occurs the meeting around the stove, the goblet for the chalice, "Weshail" for the "Dominus vobiscum," "Drinkheill" for the "Et cum spiritu tuo."[73]

How these revels began and proceeded may be indicated in the 1350 *Speculum*'s Book II, chapter 38, "On Drunkenness." Ranulph says clearly that clerics ought not encourage each other to imbibe, nor should they match each other drink for drink, nor—as they gorge themselves—ought they question the honor of some of the saints, nor—during feasts or in stage plays—ought the saints be made laughable.[74] Because of their colorful nature, these comments about the destruction wrought by gluttony may have been occasioned by Higden's personal experience.

The equally destructive behavior that turned monasteries into bordellos doubtless affected his intransigent position, as stated in the *Speculum*'s later version, on the vow of continence "from which even the pope cannot dispense [release from obligation] because it can hardly be commuted into a better good."[75] Although he acknowledges that differences of opinion do occur about this matter, he still concludes that "since the requirement of continence—which is repugnant to matrimony—is essential to the status of religious life, it seems that in a vow, solemnized by religious profession, the church cannot dispense [from obligation]."[76] He is likewise definitive in maintaining that obedience is the greatest of religious vows because it offers a person's will to God; this is "preferable to the body, which is itself offered through chastity or to temporal goods which are offered through poverty."[77] Following long-standing tradition, in the *Speculum*'s second book (*On the Sins*) the serious problem of disobedience is treated as a species of pride, the premier deadly sin. There, in chapter 11, a terse statement identifies "rebellion which despises everything" as

---

[73] Fol. 103v: "Item sicut in templo fiunt laudaciones vigilie et obsequia, sic gulosis loco inuitatorii sunt inuitaciones ad potandum, loco leccionum fabulaciones iniquorum, loco responsoriorum verba caucionum, loco psalmorum adulaciones et detracciones, pro geniculacionibus sunt adiuraciones in genibus ad potandum, loco processionis fit conductus circa caminum, ciphus pro calice, 'Weshail' pro 'Dominus vobiscum,' 'Drinkheill' pro 'Et cum spiritu tuo.'"

[74] Fol. 105v: "Set et potissime clerici non debent se mutuo cohortari ad bibendum, vel ad sumendum potus equales … nec debent rogare in honorem aliquorum sanctorum vt se ingurgitent, nec in conuiuiis aut spectaculis debent ioculares fieri." Little wonder that Higden ends chapter 39 ("About the Remedies for Gluttony") with six scriptural quotations which use some form of the adjective "sobrius"; see fol. 107r.

[75] Fol. 29r: "Item papa non dispensat contra solempne votum continencie quia vix posset comutari [sic] in melius bonum."

[76] Ibid.: "quia debitum continencie est essenciale statui religionis quod repugnat matrimonio videtur quod in voto solempnizato per professionem religionis non possit ecclesia dispensare." Dispensation or a releasing from obligation is discussed frequently in Book I of the later *Speculum*.

[77] Ibid.: "Per illud aliquid maius Deo offertur, scilicet, ipsa voluntas que pocior est quam ipsum corpus quod offertur per castitatem vel quam bona temporalia que offeruntur per paupertatem."

pride's tenth level.[78] In the chapter previous, "On the Daughters of Pride," Ranulph had also handled disobedience. Citing 1 Kings 15 [:23], he relates it to idolatry, agreeing with Anselm that the font of all evil is man's own will.[79] Underlining its gravity, especially "against the commands of spiritual fathers," he mentions that death was sometimes its punishment.[80] Since the disruptions of contention and discord are explained next, presumably this "death" is spiritual, not physical, in nature. Nevertheless, Ranulph's dissatisfaction with conditions in Chester is signaled here since disobedience is the only daughter of pride for which a penalty is assessed.

At the end of chapter 28, "Concerning the Fifth Commandment: You Shall Not Kill" in the 1350 *Speculum*'s first book, Ranulph, perhaps unwittingly, reveals another grave concern. He had been discussing whether or not church leaders were obliged to remain at their posts during persecutions, thus risking their lives. He opines that if the persecutors are intent solely on pillaging the goods of the church, "faith and justice being saved, it is not necessary that superiors expose themselves to death."[81] The circumstances in which the opposite course of action must be embraced forms what should have been the chapter's conclusion: "As Ambrose said to the Emperor Theodosius: 'if you rape, if you devour, I will bear it; if you touch the sanctuary, there you will find the priest.'"[82] To this bold statement, however, Ranulph has appended a query only tangentially related to the above discussion and not actually answered: "What if once good subordinates rise up against a superior, is there still hope of conversion?"[83] Perhaps he was specifically thinking of Ralph de Chaddesden, a ringleader of the opposition to Abbot Bebington, who subsequently became an apostate religious and whose arrest was "signified"—probably by a type of bench warrant—on October 15, 1351.[84] In this case, there would definitely be a

---

[78] Fol. 76r: "Decimus gradus est rebellio que omnes contempnit."

[79] Fol. 73v: "fons tocius mali propria hominis voluntas." Although this statement was a commonplace in church doctrine for many centuries (at least since Augustine), Ranulph cites Anselm probably because of St. Werburgh's initial connection to Bec-Hellouin and by reason of Benedictine camaraderie.

[80] Ibid.: "Idcirco, propter eius grauedinem, pena aliquando fuit mors .... De penis, vero, inobediencium contra iussa patrum spiritualium dicit in secundo libro *Dialogorum* [4.24] et in *Vitis patrum* et Deut. 8 [:20] dicitur: 'vos peribitis si inobedientes fueritis.'" See PL 77:356.

[81] Fol. 40r: "Si autem persequtores solummodo querant res ecclesie salua fide et iusticia non est necesse vt prelati ad mortem se exponant."

[82] Ibid.: "Sicut dixit Ambrosius ad Imperatorem Theodosium: 'si rapis, si deuoras sustinebo; si ad sanctuarium manuum extenderis, ibi sacerdotem reperies.'" The quotation seems to affirm that the Emperor can get away with many abusive practices but will not be allowed to touch anything central to the faith.

[83] Ibid.: "Quod si subditi insurgunt in prelatum quamdiu fuerint ibi boni et spes est de conuersione."

[84] Logan, *Runaway Religious*, 191.

negative answer to the question, but Ranulph may not have been sure how negative in late 1350.

This chapter's final sentence seems to equate those opposed to a superior with persecutors of the church. Suggesting a viable course of action in such a circumstance, Higden says: "The shepherd should not desert them but, if all should prove incorrigible and the persecution is inextinguishable, then he can desert them."[85] Whether the foregoing constitutes advice to Bebington to flee or whether it is a warning to an incoming abbot about difficulties at the monastery cannot be determined; conceivably its admonitory tone affected the discussion of scandal as spiritual homicide in the following chapter.

For Higden, who tends to be very careful about interfering with good order and the absolute nature of truth, weighing whether veracity can be slighted because of scandal cannot have been a happy endeavor. He situates, among the actions associated with the pursuit of truth, a superior's exercise of correction and instruction and laments that this is sometimes avoided because of numbers and lack of opportunity, especially if all subordinates are obstinate and no conversion may entirely be hoped for.[86] When he penned these remarks, the objections of most of the monks to the self-serving actions of Abbot Bebington might not yet have resulted in any disastrous consequences, but Ranulph seems already pessimistic about overcoming the trend toward rebellious behavior. The numbers involved might also have discouraged and disillusioned him, as did the abrogation of an official ban imposed on clerics for serious transgressions "because so many were guilty."[87]

The fact that St. Werburgh's was experiencing a period of religious and governmental disruption gives additional force to Ranulph's protracted discussion of charity in the later version's Book I, chapter 47. He sees it, first, as diminished in fervor through the cessation of good works because, at that point "for subordinates, facility in obeying superiors is lessened."[88] Concupiscence and confusion are also agents of charity's diminishment, especially since "so many retrogress and become tepid after great fervor."[89] The monastery's troubles are further indicated by Ranulph's extensive

---

[85] Fol. 40r: "Pastor non debet eos deserere set si omnes sint incorrigibiles et persequcio est inextinguibilis, tunc potest eos deserere."

[86] Fol. 40v: "Tercia est veritas discipline correccionis [fol. 41r] vel doctrine pertinens ad prelatum que aliquando dimittenda est propter multitudinem aut propter non opportunitatem, vt si omnes subditi essent obstinati et nulla omnino speraretur conuersio."

[87] Fol. 40v: "propter multitudinem labencium."

[88] Fol. 57v: "nam tunc minuitur facilitas obediendi in viribus inferioribus erga superiores."

[89] Ibid.: "… crescit cupiditas et minuitur caritas … sicut contingit fieri de inperfecto perfectum sic e contrario eo quod multi retrocedant et fiunt post magnum feruorem tepidi."

treatment of fraternal correction—announced as the twelfth evangelical counsel in chapter 48 and given extensive treatment throughout the whole of chapter 49.

Fraternal correction—a process that includes exposing personal faults and breaches in monastic discipline, as well as offering remedies to cure and prevent them—was commonplace in theological discussion during the central and later Middle Ages.[90] Ranulph himself handled it competently (fols. 31r to 32v in the Durham MS.) in the 1340 version of the *Speculum*. It is intriguing to look at the manuscripts that transmit the earlier recension at this juncture. All announce in chapter 17, "On Fraternal Correction," that the reader should consult ("vide infra") advisory commentary in either chapter 48 or chapter 49 under the section labeled *Doctorem* to ascertain "how an authority ought to act with regard to correction."[91] But, this matter—the twelfth point under fraternal correction in the 1350 text—is treated in neither of the referenced chapters of the earlier edition (which actually deal with the sacrament of holy orders); the later recension, as well, adds a thirteenth point not found anywhere in the 1340 version: "What Is to Be Done When the Superior Is the Offender."[92] Because all of the surviving manuscripts that preserve the first version were written well after 1350[93] and are not copies of each other,[94] it is possible that the scribes who transmitted the 1340 exemplar had both earlier and later, or even different, transcriptions at hand when they wrote that "vide infra." It is also possible that a need for more commentary on fraternal correction was perceived and/ or hoped for by later copyists and that a chapter on who should be ordained might deal with excluding consistent offenders. That all four manuscripts of the 1340 edition include the reference to this missing advice about correction may be further evidence about deteriorating discipline at St. Werburgh's.

Aside from the puzzling direction noted above, fraternal correction is treated more clearly in the later edition than in 1340, even though much of the same material appears in both, including Augustine's dictum that if you neglect to correct your brother, you are dragged down by him.[95] The 1350 recension's clarity results from

---

[90] Alexander of Hales laid the theological groundwork for the development of this topic; Thomas Aquinas built on it in *Summa theologica* 2-2, qu. 33, art. 1 and 2. Ranulph's definition (fol. 59v) is similar to that of Aquinas: "correpcio fraterna est admonicio fratris super emendacione delicti ex superna fraterna caritate proueniens" ("Fraternal correction, modeled on fraternal love in heaven, is the admonition of a brother about emending a fault").

[91] In the Durham MS. the chapter number is 48; in the three others, it is 49. The word *Doctorem* does not occur at any point in the chapter (49) on fraternal correction in the 1350 edition.

[92] Fol. 59v: "Tercio decimo quid sit faciendum quando superior est criminosus."

[93] See the catalog pages cited in note 5.

[94] According to the stemma in Crook, "New Version," 44.

[95] From Augustine's *Sermo LXXXII* 4 (PL 38:508).

an initial, developmentally ordered listing of the thirteen major points to be handled; the control provided by this list makes the discussion both more easily accessible and logically compelling.[96] Starting with a succinct definition of the topic—missing in the 1340 version—Ranulph ponders sequentially and at some length the scope and different types of correction, when and in what order it should be performed, where the transgressions of the brothers ought to be revealed, whether correction can ever be omitted, and who should correct. He is certain that correction can and should occur, not only among the brothers and by authority, but also when subordinates sharply correct superiors who endanger the faith.[97] Endangering the faith was probably not intentional in the early-to-mid-fourteenth-century abbots of Chester and, because it is an extremely serious but rare cause for correction, would probably never be a reason to place any abbot in a compromising situation. That the phrase appears as a qualifier in the above discussion suggests that Ranulph was comfortable with a generally traditional position. Such a vantage point, combined with the distress caused by the monks who rebelled against Abbot Bebington in 1346 and took their case to the Black Prince, may have occasioned his rather harsh observation that "if [a sinner] has numerous companions and scandal is not feared, there is no sparing those associates."[98] Ranulph also sees no value in concealing wrongdoing; perhaps he was thinking of the reprehensible behavior of the monks described in the later *Speculum*'s Book II, chapter 47, or of the attack on a duly elected abbot as occurred with Richard Seynesbury in 1350. He says clearly that in cases where public disgrace or intractable suspicion exist, the superior may, "in the manner in which a civil or ecclesiastical judge can exact an oath to tell the truth, issue binding direction," presumably so that the sorry facts be revealed.[99]

In the 1350 text, the culmination of the forty-ninth chapter's description of the numerous other instances in which correction is desirable and useful is a discussion (the eleventh major point on the list) about whether any sinner is worthy to correct anyone in any way. In answer, Ranulph concludes that since everyone is an actual or potential sinner, only when one is in sin, or has committed a greater sin, or will

---

[96] For example, both versions agree that correction is enjoined by precept and then proceed differently: the 1350 version asks and answers the logical next question about whether correction pertains to everyone, while the 1340 text embarks upon a distracting discussion of three occasions on which correction can be omitted—a subject treated ninth in 1350; see fol. 59v and fols. 61v–62r in the Illinois text and fol. 31r in Durham, Dean and Chapter Library, MS. B.iv.36.

[97] Fol. 59v: "Set si immineret periculum fidei eciam prelati a subditis forent seuere corripiendi."

[98] Fol. 60r: "Si habet multitudinem sociam et scandalum non timetur, non est parcendum multitudini."

[99] Fol. 61r: "Puta per infamiam vel per suspicionem violentam aut probabilem in quibus potest prelatus precipere et modo quo iudex ciuilis vel ecclesiasticus potest exigere iuramentum de veritate dicenda."

cause scandal, or will fall victim to pride should the correction process be impeded.[100] The only absolute requirement in the corrector is humility:

> Therefore, let us consider when we correct anyone if his vice is the kind we have never had; then let us ponder that we are men and could have had it. If formerly we have had such a failing, let us recall our fragility and let us act more mildly.[101]

Although the development of this eleventh topic does not contain specific references to the troubling events in Chester, its strong emphasis on the necessity for correction sets the stage for the twelfth and thirteenth. The veiled and not-so-veiled allusions to the monastery's deteriorating state may have motivated Ranulph to accord the twelfth topic an entire chapter (50). Under the guise of investigating how an authority should proceed against an offender, he begins chapter 50 very abruptly, by discussing the distressing operations of suspicion, report, rumor, and crime.[102] The distaste associated with these four words obviates any vestige of the reasonable and sometimes positive attitude indicated in chapter 49. In addition, the fact that he felt impelled to define and illustrate these topics, thus validating and imposing some kind of order upon them, suggests that the aura of illicit intrigue at the monastery was quite palpable. The negative ambiance develops as the process of compurgation, and the attendant possibility of perjury, is discussed.[103]

Compurgation—or swearing that you are innocent and then having others swear that they believe you—is inherently unsettling and fosters a sense of uncertainty. Ranulph reifies this by his culminating exploration of notorious crime.[104] The word "notorious" had appeared previously in the chapter on "Scandal as Spiritual Homicide," but it was there associated with sin, not with crime.[105] In this venue, what is

---

[100] Fol. 62r: "Quia per peccatum redditur quis indignus ad corripiendum presertim si maius peccatum commisit … propter scandalum … propter superbiam …."

[101] Ibid.: "Idcirco cogitemus cum quemquam corripimus si tale sit eius vicium quale numquam habuimus tunc cogitemus nos homines esse et habere potuisse. Si aliquando tale habuimus, recolamus fragilitatem nostram et micius agamus."

[102] His usual pattern of development consists in presenting the idea to be discussed and dividing it into segments through a series of questions. At the end of fol. 62r, he abandons his customary introductory mode, and chapter 50 commences with the following unadorned Latin statement: "Lex tradit quod aut laborat contra criminosum suspicio aut fama aut rumor aut crimen" ("The law provides that there operates against the person arraigned either suspicion, or report, or rumor, or crime").

[103] On fol. 62v.

[104] Fol. 63v: "de crimine notorio est sciendum quod aliud est notorium iuris, aliud facti, aliud est notorium presumptum."

[105] Fol. 40r: "Scandalum … dicitur dictum vel factum minus rectum occasionem prebens ruine; vt si sacerdos peccet notorie sumitur inde exemplum fornicandi et depreuandi statum sacerdotalem" ("Scandal … is said to be an improper pronouncement or deed affording an occasion of ruin; for example, if a priest should sin notoriously, there is thereby taken a model for fornicating and for perverting the priestly state)."

"notorious by law" is quickly dealt with; what is "notorious by fact" and "presumed notorious" is shown to be public and undeniable, just as openly practiced fornication would be public and undeniable. Those uncomfortable citations preface commentary on the necessity for evidence; Ranulph avers that, in blatantly obvious offenses, neither an accuser nor a witness must come forward.[106] Here Higden may be referring to the promiscuous behavior of his brother monks. Or, despite his penchant to be supportive of authority, he may have finally acknowledged that the abbot's depredations in the countryside had moved beyond any level of tolerance.

Putatively most revelatory would have been the thirteenth and final topic to be discussed in the first book of the *Speculum*: "What Is to Be Done When the Superior Is the Offender." This subject could have been treated as an extension of chapter 50 or could have become chapter 51, but the text breaks off after the word "nisi" at the bottom of fol. 63v, seemingly just before Ranulph undertook his explication. A torn stub indicates that the eighth or last leaf is missing from this gathering. Since Ranulph was methodical and complete in developing the subsections of his chapters, positing a sudden cessation of commentary is not supportable;[107] equally unlikely is the possibility that the last leaf was left blank. Given the fact that each page has room for 36–39 lines, there would have been sufficient space on this eighth leaf to complete chapter 50 and the projected chapter about what one should do when the person in charge is the criminal. Why this discussion is missing is a tantalizing question. Did the violence at St. Werburgh's prompt the excision? Was it the act of the copyist who could have been complicit in the violence or equally wary of its being directed at himself? Was the leaf torn out at a later time for reasons unknown?

With reference to this missing folio, the script used may be important to consider. According to Neil Ker's entry (dated "3/'69") in the Rare Book Room catalog of the University of Illinois, the *Speculum* manuscript is written in Anglicana, a type of book hand common to the third quarter of the fourteenth century. This dating makes it conceivable that the text was copied while Higden (d. 1363) was still alive and able to exercise some control over what was happening in the scriptorium. It is even possible that Ranulph himself tore out the missing folio. Nevertheless, despite this intriguing array of possibilities, the questions "by whom" and "for what specific reason" the folio was deliberately removed must remain matters for conjecture.

When the *Speculum* achieved its final form, Ranulph was an old man with his world to lose. Although, in the later Middle Ages, some Benedictine houses sought

---

[106] Fol. 63v: "nec requiritur accusator nec testis."

[107] Scribal error is the likely cause of the three discrepancies in the whole of Book I of the *Speculum*. In chapter 10, Ranulph announces ten degrees of superstition, though nine are discussed; in chapter 38, both the sixth and eleventh points are omitted.

to reappropriate their religious traditions and others—like St. Cuthbert's in Durham—remained consistently prosperous and stable,[108] by 1350, the prognosis for the future well-being of Higden's monastery might not have seemed promising to him, and in this he would have been eminently correct.

Because of his numerous attacks on nearby religious establishments—some under the "protection" of the abbey—Richard Seynesbury was forcibly removed as abbot in 1362, the year before Ranulph died; he refused obedience to his successor, who was only marginally better, and left St. Werburgh's without permission in 1368.[109] In 1382, the signatures appended to an important deed indicate that only twenty-four monks resided at the monastery; a decade later the abbot of Tewkesbury informed the chapter that the number of resident monks was insufficient.[110]

Even more disturbing is the case of Thomas de Yardley, who apostatized from Chester about 1400 and was accused of abducting and robbing a female pilgrim on her way home from Walsingham, for which he was arrested. Thomas was returned to St. Werburgh's and, on April 5, 1412, he was "pardoned for treasons, felonies, misprisions, rapes, rebellions, depredations, robberies, contempts, offenses, lying in ambush, murder, common larceny, and other trespasses."[111] In 1413, he became abbot.

Certainly, the critique in the later *Speculum* makes Higden seem almost prescient about the unfortunate history of St. Werburgh's in the fifty years after his death. But does his caustic and often mournful commentary allow for any general conclusions about the status of monasteries in England after the Great Plague, or about the relationship of prescriptive/normative literature—especially the manual of instruction—to events within religious communities other than Chester? The answer to both queries appears to be in the negative.

Chester was one of many abbeys experiencing a sharp decline around 1350; the principal cause of its deterioration, however, was unique. Whereas some monasteries suffered catastrophic losses in terms of personnel and financing as a result of the Black Death, St. Werburgh's seems to have been the victim of a different kind of plague—one initiated in violence and fostered by drunkenness and incontinence. And, unlike other foundations that did not recover from the blows of the mid-fourteenth century, by the mid-fifteenth Chester's fortunes were again on the rise;

---

[108] Nicholas Heale, "Rottenness and Renewal in the Later Medieval Monasteries," in *Monks of England*, ed. Daniel Rees (London, 1997), 135–47 (here 147), and R. Dobson, *Durham Priory: 1400–1450* (Cambridge, 1973), 55.

[109] Logan, *Runaway Religious*, 192.

[110] Knowles and Hadcock, *Religious Houses*, 62 and Pantin, *Documents*, 2:92.

[111] Logan, *Runaway Religious*, 193.

it was attractive enough to the reformers in 1541 to survive as one of only four monastic installations to become cathedral churches.[112]

As Chester cannot lay claim to exemplar status in terms of monastic life, neither can the structure, contents, or relationships of the 1350 *Speculum curatorum* be seen as a model for the practice of similar manuals of instruction. Like the *Ars componendi sermones* (mentioned earlier), the *Speculum* is the only text of its kind to have been authored by a Benedictine. Moreover, a survey of works in the same genre reveals a more significant way in which its singularity can be demonstrated. William of Doune's *Memoriale presbyterorum* (1343) is "devoted solely to confessional technique"; it puts its many constituencies on trial in order to achieve social discipline or the right ordering of society on a model of inflexible moral principles.[113] William of Pagula's *Oculus sacerdotis* (1320–1328) reviews nearly every aspect of systematic and moral theology, but it and the *Cilium oculi* and *Regimen animarum* (1342) demonstrate great concern about confessional and penitential procedures, desiring to instruct the cleric who must administer the sacrament, evaluate the nature and gravity of sins confessed, and assign an appropriate punishment.[114] Ranulph's *Speculum* takes a different tack, one signaled by the most noticeable expansion in the second edition. Whereas the 1340 text had devoted just one chapter (4 folios, 6r to 10r in the Durham manuscript) to the topic of the commandments, by 1350 the Decalogue occupies 63 folios. Such a dramatic change indicates an important shift in orientation—away from legislation and moralization and toward catechesis. In his greatly revised manual, Ranulph expounds Christian doctrine to what he fears—and perhaps knows—is a poorly prepared audience and, even in his discussion of penance, the emphasis is not primarily on the punishment to be meted out, but on the nature of this sacrament and on the actions necessary to insure a "metanoya" or change of heart: fasting, alms-giving, and prayer.[115] As a corollary to and consequence of his presentation about what constitutes the Christian life, Higden faces the failures and shortcomings of his brother monks, exposing these to view and, in hope, to correction. The revelation is personal and particular, not paradigmatic. That it was also deeply troubling to him as an eyewitness is sadly clear.

---

[112] *VCH Ches.* 5, 88–9.

[113] Michael Haren, *Sin and Society in Fourteenth-Century England* (Oxford, 2000), 1, 5.

[114] The most comprehensive review of the medieval manuals of instruction is found in the unpublished D.Phil. dissertation of Leonard E. Boyle, "A Survey of the Writings Attributed to William of Pagula" (Oxford, 1956), vol. 1. See also idem, "The *Oculus sacerdotis* and Some Other Works of William of Pagula," in *Pastoral Care*, 4:82–5.

[115] Fols. 258v–263r.

Bibliography of Margaret Jennings

Books

1. *Tutivillus: The Literary Career of the Recording Demon*, Studies in Philology, Studies and Texts 74:5 (Chapel Hill, N.C.: University of North Carolina Press, 1977).
2. *The Ars componendi sermones of Ranulph Higden, O.S.B.*, Davis Medieval Texts and Studies 6 (Leiden: Brill, 1991).
3. (with Sally A. Wilson:) *Ranulph Higden, Ars componendi sermones*, Dallas Medieval Texts and Translations 2 (Louvain: Peeters. 2003).
4. (with Eugene Crook:) *Ranulph Higden, Speculum curatorum—A Mirror for Curates*, Book I: *The Commandments*, Dallas Medieval Texts and Translations 13:1 (Louvain: Peeters. 2012).
5. (with Eugene Crook:) *Ranulph Higden, Speculum curatorum—A Mirror for Curates*, Book II: *The Capital Sins*, Dallas Medieval Texts and Translations 13:2 (Louvain: Peeters, 2016).

Articles and Reviews

1. "The Art of the Pseudo-Origen Homily *De Maria Magdalena*," *Medievalia et Humanistica* N.S. 5 (1974): 139–52.
2. "Lucan's Medieval Popularity: The Exemplum Tradition," *Revista di Cultura Classica e Medioevale* 16 (1974): 215–33.
3. "Richard Rolle and the Three Degrees of Love," *Downside Review* 93:312 (1975): 193–200.
4. "Bartleby the Existentialist," *Extracts: An Occasional Newsletter* 22 (May 1975): 8–10.
5. "Chaucer's Troilus and the Ruby," *Notes & Queries* 23:12 (1976): 533–7.
6. "Typological Dialectic in Milton's Major Poems," *Forum* 17:2 (Spring 1976): 16–22.
7. "Parabola: Hart Crane and Existentialism," *The Markham Review* 5 (Winter 1976): 31–4.
8. "Monks and the *Artes Praedicandi* in the Time of Ranulph Higden," *Revue bénédictine* 86 (1976): 119–28.

9. "Higden's Minor Writings and the Fourteenth-Century Church," *Proceedings of the Leeds Philosophical and Literary society, Literary and Historical Section* 16:7 (1977): 149–58.

10. "Monks and the *Artes Praedicandi* in the Time of Ranulph Higden: An Acknowledgement," *Revue bénédictine* 87 (1977): 389–90.

11. "Chaucer's Beards," *Archiv für das Studium der neueren Sprachen und Literaturen* 215 (1978): 362–8.

12. "Piers Plowman and Holychurch," *Viator* 9 (1978): 367–74.

13. "The *Ars componendi sermones* of Ranulph Higden," in *Medieval Eloquence: Studies in the Theory and Practice of Medieval Rhetoric*, ed. James Jerome Murphy (Berkeley: University of California Press, 1978), 122–6.

14. (with Eugene Crook:) "The Devil and Ranulph Higden," *Manuscripta* 22 (1978): 131–40.

15. "The Isolatoes in Melville's *Clarel*," *American Notes & Queries* 18:4 (December 1979): 53–6.

16. "Ars moriendi. B. Literatur. III. Mittelenglische Literatur," in *Lexikon des Mittelalters*, vol. 1 (Munich: Artemis, 1980), cols. 1042–3.

17. (with Beryl Rowland:) "Medieval Multiple Birth," *Neuphilologische Mitteilungen* 81:2 (1980): 169–73.

18. (with Eugene Crook:) "Grading Sin: A Medieval English Benedictine in the *cura animarum*," *American Benedictine Review* 31 (1980): 335–45.

19. "'Heavens Defend Me from that Welsh Fairy' (*Merry Wives of Windsor*, V,5,85): the Metamorphosis of Morgain la Fee in the Romances," in *Court and Poet: Selected Proceedings. Third Congress of the International Courtly Literature Society*, ed. Glyn S. Burgess (Liverpool: Francis Cairns, 1981), 197–205.

20. "Ironic Dancing Absolon in the *Miller's Tale*," *Florilegium* 5 (1983): 178–88.

21. (with Beryl Rowland:) "Unheavenly Twins," *Neuphilologische Mitteilungen* 85:1 (1984): 108–14.

22. "To Pryke or to Prye: Scribal Delights in the *Troilus*, Book III," in *Chaucer in the Eighties*, ed. Julian N. Wasserman and Robert J. Blanch (Syracuse, N.Y.: Syracuse University Press, 1986), 121–33.

23. "In Search of Structure: Remembrance of Things Past," *The Antioch Review* 45:3 (Summer 1987): 298–302.

24. (collator for *Troilus* text:) *Riverside Chaucer*, ed. Larry D. Benson (New York: Houghton-Mifflin, 1987).

25. "'Rhetor Redivivus?' Cicero in the 'Artes praedicandi,'" *Archives d'histoire doctrinale et littéraire du moyen âge* 56 (1989): 91–122.

26. "Review of *Listener's Guide to Medieval English: A Discography*, by Betsy Bowden," *Speculum* 65:4 (October 1990): 947–9.

27. "Structure in *Christ III*," *Neuphilologische Mitteilungen* 92:4 (1991): 445–55.

28. "*Non ex virgine*: Rise of the Thematic Preaching Manual," *Collegium Medievale* 5 (1992): 27–44.

29. "The 'Sermons' of English Romance," *Florilegium* 13 (1994): 121–40.

30. "Review Essay: *St. Katherine of Alexander: The Late Middle English Prose Legend in Southwell Minster MS 7*, ed. by Saara Nevanlinna and Irma Taavitsainen," *Florilegium* 13 (1994): 173–5.

31. "Rood and Ruthwell: The Power of Paradox," *English Language Notes* 31:3 (1994): 6–12.

32. "Review of *Parabolaire*, by Galand de Reigny, ed. and trans. Colette Friedlander, Dom Jean Leclercq, Gaetano Raciti," *Speculum* 69:3 (July 1994): 772–3.

33. "Medieval Themes in Modern British and American Literature: Alive and Well," *The European Legacy* 1:3 (1996): 1140–5.

34. "Review of *Sermones*, by Thomas de Chobham, ed. Franco Morenzoni," *Speculum* 71:3 (1996): 768–70.

35. (with Francis P. Kilcoyne:) "Rethinking 'Continuity': Erasmus' *Ecclesiastes* and the *Artes Praedicandi*," *Renaissance and Reformation/Renaissance et Réforme* 33:4 (1997): 5–24.

36. "Like Shining from Shook Foil: Liturgical Typology in Hrotsvit's Legends and Dramas," *Mittellateinisches Jahrbuch* 33:1 (1998): 37–52.

37. "Review of *Devils, Women and Jews: Reflections of the Other in Medieval Sermon Stories*, by Joan Young Gregg," *Speculum* 73:4 (1998): 1142.

38. "The Three Marys of Bourges," *Downside Review* 119:414 (2001): 35–50.

39. "Prophecy in Glass and Stone: Jewish Influences on the Cathedral of Bourges," in *Insights and Interpretations: Studies in Celebration of the Eighty-Fifth Anniversary of the Index of Christian Art*, ed. Colum Hourihane (Princeton, N.J.: Princeton University Press, 2002), 182–210.

40. (with Francis P. Kilcoyne:) "Defacement: Practical Theology, Politics, or Prejudice. The Case of the North Portal at Bourges," *Church History* 72:2 (June 2003): 276–303.

41. "Beryl Rowland: In Memoriam," *The Chaucer Review* 38 (2004): 203–04.

42. "Eyewitness: Ranulph Higden and the Disturbing Events at Chester Monastery," *The Journal of Medieval and Renaissance History*, 3rd series, vol. 7 (2010): 167–93.